S·U·P·E·R·C·A·R·S

LOTUS ESPRIT TURBO

F250 XNG

JOHN SIMISTER

a Salamander book

Published by Salamander Books Limited
LONDON • NEW YORK

A SALAMANDER BOOK

Published by Salamander Books Ltd,
52 Bedford Row,
London WC1R 4LR

© Salamander Books Ltd, 1989

ISBN 0 86101 441 3

Distributed in the United Kingdom by
Hodder & Stoughton Services,
P.O. Box 6, Mill Road,
Dunton Green, Sevenoaks,
Kent TN13 2XX

Editor: Richard Collins

Designer: Paul Johnson

Line diagrams: Maltings Partnership
(© Salamander Books Ltd)

Colour profile: Maltings Partnership
(© Salamander Books Ltd)

Filmset by Copyset Ltd

Colour reproduction by Scantrans, Singapore

Printed in Italy

Acknowledgements

My grateful thanks go to: Ian Adcock, Lotus
Public Relations Manager and former *Motor*
colleague, for arranging interviews, lending cars,
opening the archives and more; Mike Kimberley,
Tony Rudd, Colin Spooner and Roger Becker for
so willingly sparing time to talk; to Stuart Ellis
for showing how a Lotus Esprit is made; to the
ghost of *Motor* for performance figures and the
chance to drive earlier Esprits; to Jeremy Walton,
Graham Robson and Jabby Crombac for their
earlier words on Lotus and the Esprit; and to my
wife Deborah without whose encouragement this
book might never have been written.

Contents

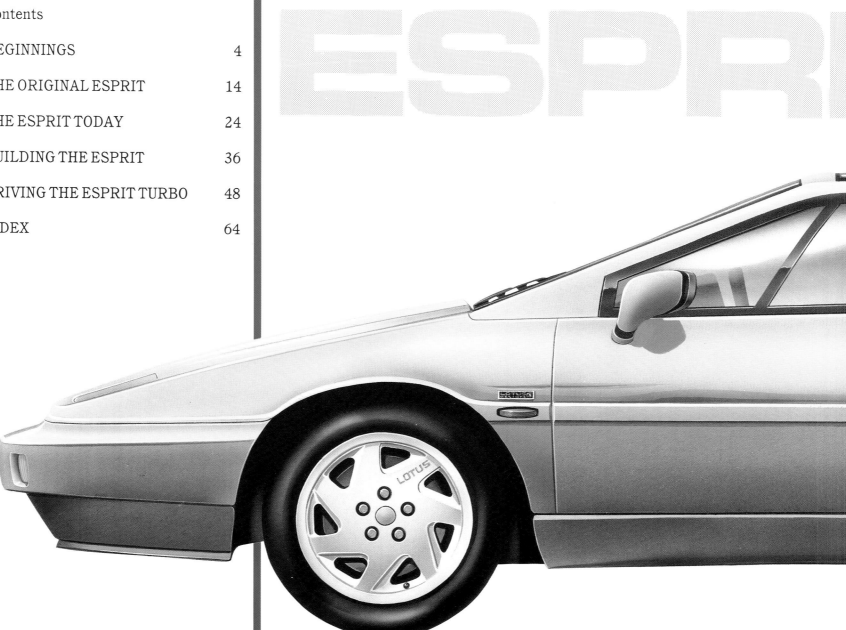

INTRODUCTION

If ever a car manufacturer was upwardly mobile, it is Lotus. In 1948, the first Lotus was a backyard special based on a pre-war Austin Seven. In 1989, the latest intercooled Lotus Esprit Turbo is capable of nearly 170mph, while cossetting its driver in leather-clad luxury.

Between these two extremes lies a rich and often turbulent history, a history made on the race track as much as the road. For we must not forget that Lotus, a fully paid-up member of the roadgoing supercar club, has won the Formula One Constructors' Championship seven times, and its cars have powered their drivers to six World Drivers' Championships. Nowadays Team Lotus has little to do with the road cars that share the green and yellow badge, but for many years both road cars and racers bore the hallmarks of the same man's vision.

That man was Colin Chapman, the Lotus founder whose life was cut short by a heart attack in 1982. Chapman was an innovator, a single-minded man who disliked compromise. When the world fuel crisis threatened to kill his plans for an all-new model range he kept faith in his judgement; now, the fruits of that foresight can be seen in today's desireable Lotuses, directly descended from that all-new family.

Colin Chapman is gone, but his company continues to function according to the philosophies he laid down. The new Elan, when it appears, is poised to set new standards just as its 1962 namesake did. Lotus's most exciting car, the latest Esprit Turbo, retains much of the flavour of the original 1975 Esprit, but has come of age in just the same way as the company that makes it.

Don't think, however, that Lotus's maturity will breed complacency. Indeed, the future has never looked brighter. The intercooled Esprit Turbo SE brings Lotus performance to new heights; a turbocharged Excel is likely to follow. The all-new, front-wheel-drive Elan is the car that will return Lotus to the market sector which, with hindsight, the company should never have abandoned; it will set standards just as its ancestor did.

Meanwhile, the Lotus Esprit Turbo – blisteringly fast, with impeccable handling and styling as tastefully restrained as that of a mid-engined supercar can be – is the British reply to the products of Ferrari and Porsche. It also encapsulates the very essence of Lotus, the high-technology company with the sports car heritage.

BEGINNINGS

State-of-the-art sports cars and World Championship-winning racing cars: an impeccable pedigree

THE FOLLOWING FACT may surprise you. Lotus has been making cars for barely a year less than Ferrari; the 40th anniversary was celebrated in 1988. The Esprit, subject of this book, has occupied the last thirteen years of the surprisingly long, and enormously eventful, history of the Lotus marque. In doing so, it encapsulates the very essence of Lotus today – a company which has emerged from the dark days of financial uncertainty and the sudden death of its founder and visionary, Colin Chapman, into a healthy enterprise making some of the world's most desirable cars and whose engineering and design expertise is in demand the world over.

THE FAMILY TREE
Europa – and earlier
The Esprit, announced in October 1975 with the turbocharged version following five years later, has one obvious ancestor: the Europa. With the Europa it shares its mid-engined layout, its backbone chassis, its seating capacity for two and its glassfibre-reinforced plastic bodywork. Yet the Esprit is a larger, faster, more expensive, more prestigious car, designed to fill a slot upmarket of the Europa's in a section of the market then new to Lotus.

So it is that the Esprit owes much, too, to a car with its engine at the front; the second-generation Elite, first of the present family of Lotus cars and whose direct descendant, the Excel, is not only still made but keeps on getting better and better. To the Elite can be traced the Esprit's injection-moulded body production process and its all-aluminium, twin-cam, 16-valve, Lotus-designed and built engine.

To put these two forebears into perspective, though, we must slip back further in time. To a time, in fact, when Lotuses emerged not from a spacious factory in rural Norfolk, but from an adapted stable block behind Colin Chapman's father's pub next to a railway line in Hornsey, north London. Here, the Lotus Engineering Company was inaugurated on 1 January 1952. Chapman had already caused his earliest stirs among the motor racing establishment, beginning in 1948 with a much-modified Austin Seven which was the first car to bear the Lotus name. Why Lotus? That is a question which has never been answered.

Lotuses Mark I to IV (the switch to Arabic numerals came later, with the 11 sports racing car) were all Austin-based, and the V was never built. The VI's chassis, however, was pure Lotus and it was this car that set Chapman up as a proper, albeit small-scale, car manufacturer and prompted the formation of the company that was later to change its name to Lotus Cars Limited. An improved version of that car, the Lotus VII or Seven, was launched at the 1957 Earl's Court Motor Show although Lotus racing car type numbers were by then well into double figures. Thirty-one years on the Seven is still made, by Caterham Car Sales who bought the manufacturing rights from Lotus in 1973, Low, light, rudimentary and rapid, little more than an engine, a space-frame chassis, two seats and four wheels, this is the car so often described as a four-wheeled motorcycle.

BIRTH OF THE ELITE
The first Lotus GT
The Seven, in truth, was effectively a racing car which could be used on the road. However, that 1957 Motor Show also saw the debut of the car that sowed the seed of the family tree whose freshest fruits are today's Esprit and Excel. That car was the Lotus 14, or Elite; not the Elite referred to earlier, which ushered in a new era for Lotus in 1974 with its 16-valve engine and four seats, but the original Elite with chassis-less, monocoque glassfibre construction.

That show car was little more than a very convincing mock-up, for it had no running gear. Yet the delicacy of its curvaceous lines approached perfection. The Elite look, with proportions so right that the car didn't look the diminutive machine it was, is usually attributed to amateur stylist and professional money-man Peter Kirwan-Taylor. But he should not take all the credit. Aerodynamicist Frank Costin perfected the cut-off tail to improve airflow; three moonlighters from Ford came up with that idea in the first place, and carried out much of the detail work

Below: The Lotus Europa, seen here in S2 form, was the Esprit's most obvious ancestor. Like the Esprit it had a mid-mounted engine and two seats, as well as other Lotus traits like glassfibre bodywork and a backbone chassis. Its handling and roadholding were greatly admired at the time, its performance less so.

including the making of models and the prototype body. One of those moonlighters, Ron Hickman, was later to make his fortune by designing the Black and Decker Workmate; another, John Frayling, styled the ill-fated Clan Crusader of 1970.

The Elite never saw the inside of a wind tunnel, yet such was the aerodynamic efficiency of its shape that its drag coefficient was later measured at just 0.29. No more than a handful of modern cars can match that degree of slipperiness. The car was also very light, having a minimum of metalwork beneath its plastic skin, so despite an engine of just 1216cc it was disarmingly rapid. That the engine came from Coventry Climax, manufacturers of fire-pump engines which happened to go particularly well in racing cars, helped; it was a classic all-aluminium, single overhead-camshaft design, built in a special FWE (Feather Weight Elite) version specifically for the Elite.

Getting the Elite into production was fraught with difficulties. There was minimal space at the Hornsey 'works', and innumerable problems surrounded the metamorphosis from show car to running, quantity-produced reality. A racing yacht builder in the south of England helped with the production engineering – if such a term can

apply to such a low-volume car – of the body, and this firm (Maximar) also made the first shells. Before any Elites so much as reached potential buyers of agile roadgoing GT cars, however, these shells were snapped up by racing teams anxious to put into practice Colin Chapman's real reason for creating the Elite.

That reason was to race it; and, in particular, to race it at Le Mans in the GT class. The Elite won the up-to-1500cc class there in 1959; and in that year, by which time Lotus had moved to a new factory in Cheshunt, Hertfordshire (on the northern outskirts of London), Elites began properly to appear on the road. Not many were made between production's tentative start in 1958 and its cessation in 1963; most experts put the figure at less than 1000 cars with a few extra monocoque body units left at the end.

There were two main reasons for the Elite's short life. A fine driver's car it might have been, a car for the purist with its functional interior and pop-out side windows, but it was very expensive even if the buyer saved on Purchase Tax by buying the car only semi-completed. It was also a demanding car to own, needing thorough and frequent servicing and not boasting a particularly enviable reliability record. Its lightweight shell

Above: Lotus's first true GT car was the original Elite of 1957, noted for its chassisless glassfibre construction and the beauty of its perfectly proportioned lines. Although fragile, Elites were fast with their Climax engines and raced with considerable success. This is Elite expert Miles Wilkins' immaculate example.

was fragile, too. Yet, despite the high price, every Elite sold lost money for Lotus. The car nearly wiped out Maximar, who managed to extricate themselves from body manufacture before they sank without trace, and even when the Bristol Aeroplane Company took over the body production later on the Elite's balance sheet remained depressingly red.

Bristol, too, made no money out of its Elite involvement. Indeed, Ron Hickman (speaking to British journalist Chris Harvey for *Supercar Classics*) reckons that the public, through the Government's Blue Streak missile contract, indirectly subsidised Bristol's part in Elite production. Clearly this could not last, and supplies of the Climax engine were running out anyway with Lotus unable to fund production of another batch, so the Elite reached the end of the road. A quarter of a century on, a good Elite is a collector's jewel; such people, nowadays, tend to be more tolerant of its temperament.

ENTER THE ELAN
Standard-setting sports car

Its replacement was a much more carefully thought-out machine. The Elan (Lotus 26), announced for the 1962 Earl's Court Motor Show, wore a particularly pretty, Hickman-styled open two-seater body which bore more than a passing resemblance to the Elite. But what lurked beneath the skin was more significant, and laid the foundation stone of Lotus chassis design from that point on: it was a tough, pressed steel backbone frame, forked at the front to carry the engine and front suspension, and at the rear to carry the differential and rear suspension. Over this the glassfibre body set saddle-fashion, the resultant assembly being rigid yet light – and far simpler to make, and more durable too, than was the Elite's glassfibre monocoque. It was also cheaper.

For the Elan to have a backbone chassis, however, was not the original intention. A glassfibre monocoque remained Chapman's desire, and it was only the difficulty of giving the structure sufficient rigidity in open form that got in the way of its adoption. Meanwhile, so that testing could go ahead on the mechanical parts, Chapman designed – at Hickman's instigation – the backbone frame, complete with high turrets at the rear to accommodate the Elite-like Chapman strut rear suspension. If Colin Chapman, ever the engineer purist, had any qualms of conscience over a design he could easily have viewed as a compromise, they were dispelled when the following year's Lotus 25 Formula 1 car was unveiled as the first monocoque single-seater. Effectively a widened backbone with the driver sat within, it helped Jim Clark to his first World Championship.

As with the chassis and body, the Elan's engine showed a more down-to-earth approach compared with its predecessor. Its block was of cast iron, and came not from a specialist racing engine manufacturer but from the Ford Motor Company. The usual home for this engine block was under the bonnet of a Cortina 1500, or a Consul Classic; installed in the Lotus, though, it flaunted an aluminium cylinder head with twin overhead camshafts, setting the pattern for all subsequent roadgoing Lotuses bar one.

This transformation from sales rep's sow's ear to sports car driver's silk purse was the work of Harry Mundy, designed during his sabbatical from full-time engine design as technical editor of *Autocar*. Strong and powerful, with a brace of 40 DCOE Weber carburettors to help the original 1499cc to an output of 100bhp, the engine was not without compromise. The water pump was in unit with the front timing cover, necessitating cylinder head removal to replace the pump; later, many Elan owners would curse this piece of engineering expediency. The original block-mounted camshaft remained *in situ* to drive the oil pump, making this in a sense a three-cam engine. And it always burnt oil (though not nearly as much as the Elite's Climax engine did).

Almost as soon as the Elan went into production, it gained an increase in capacity to 1558cc and an extra 5bhp. Indeed, what few 1499cc cars existed were converted to the new capacity retrospectively. It also gained accolade after accolade from a motoring press beside itself with enthusiasm for this extremely rapid, awesomely agile little sports car. Its cornering power, its sheer squirtability, made mainstream sports cars like the MGB (introduced at the same time) and the Triumph TR4 seem like relics from another

age. Chapman's indomitably innovative design philosophy oozed from every crevice; the Elan was one of the first cars, if not *the* first, to have retractable headlights and foam-filled impact-absorbing bumpers.

BACKBONE OF LOTUS
Europa joins Elan

By 1966, a fixed-head coupé had joined the original convertible, and numerous detail modifications had seen the Elan through S1 and S2 versions and on to S3. Of more significance to our story, though, is the launch that same year of the Europa, the mid-engined sports car that set the pattern for the Esprit.

Mid-mounted engines had become the norm for racing cars, both sports and single-seater, and to Chapman it seemed only logical to use the layout in a road car. The potential benefits of responsiveness and agility were huge, the lack of practicality unimportant because the new sports coupé was to be aimed at those who had previously bought a Lotus Seven – a car which Chapman considered over the hill (a view which hindsight does not bear out!). Thus it was intended that the car should be made by Lotus Components, the arm of the company which made the Seven, plus racing cars for customers. Team Lotus, the works racing team whose Lotus 33, driven by Jim Clark, notched up Lotus's second World Championship in 1965, was a separate entity again; over the years it would become ever more so, to the point where it eventually ceased to be part of what eventually became Group Lotus.

I mentioned earlier that there was one exception to the rule of twin cams for all Lotuses. The Europa, or Lotus 46, was that exception, for it

was powered by an all-aluminium pushrod Renault engine of 1470cc. Colin Chapman first noticed this unit at the 1964 Motor Show, fitted back-to-front, behind its gearbox, in the nose of Renault's front-wheel-drive R16. The engine had been designed so that its ancillaries were on the accessible, gearbox end, and Chapman immediately realised that it could be the perfect power plant for the Europa. It simply needed to be turned through 180° and placed behind the passenger compartment to drive the rear wheels. Put the crownwheel on the opposite side of the pinion, so that there would not be one forward gear and four reverse, tune the engine to give 82bhp, and the job would be complete.

Renault was happy to oblige, and a fringe benefit for Chapman was that Lotus would no longer be dependent on just one engine supplier (Ford). John Frayling styled a neat body, with

some resemblance to the Elan but squarer and featuring high buttresses behind the cockpit either side of the engine bay; this time there were neither pop-up headlamps nor impact-absorbing bumpers. Neither had proved particularly effective, anyway, with leaks affecting the lamps' vacuum actuation and cracks disfiguring the hard skin of the bumpers should their absorptive ability be put to the test . . .

As development, under Ron Hickman, gathered pace, it soon became clear that Chapman's dream of a simple, low-priced Seven replacement would have to remain a dream. The Europa became ever more sophisticated, a move encouraged by Lotus's fast-blossoming image as a maker of desirable, useable sports cars, and it was inevitable that it would become a mainstream model to be produced by Lotus Cars. As such, it complemented the Elan nicely, offering a

Above: The mainstay of Lotus's fortunes during the 1960s and early 1970s was the Elan, a car which set new standards of agility among sports cars. The Sprint *version of 1970, with its big-valve, 126bhp engine, was devastatingly quick as well. This Sprint is pictured in front of one of Colin Chapman's aeroplanes.*

different interpretation of a small, fast, two-seater coupé. Whether or not this overlap in appeal made sense in marketing terms, there was little doubt that the end result would be more Lotuses sold. Meanwhile, production of the Seven – mainly in kit form – continued.

Backbone chassis the Europa may have had, but it differed from the Elan in two important ways apart from the obvious one of engine position. One was the rear suspension, in which the Chapman strut gave way to what was effectively a double wishbone geometry with the fixed-length drive shaft acting as the upper link. The

Above: This Elan S3, in 115bhp Special Equipment guise, lacks the fat wheels and flared wheel arches of the later S4 and Sprint versions. Some prefer its more delicate lines. It is said that Harry Mundy's design for the Elan's twin-cam cylinder head was originally intended for the French Facel Vega company, but the firm went bankrupt.

Below: One of Mike Kimberley's first tasks, on joining Lotus from Jaguar, was to update the Europa. The result was the rapid Europa Twin-Cam, with the Elan's Lotus-Ford engine in place of the less powerful Renault unit. Cutaway rear buttresses, electric windows and adjustable seats were other welcome changes.

other was that the chassis was designed to be bonded to the body to create a single, extremely rigid unit; in practice, this was a disaster because it was practically impossible to repair properly after a major accident – or, later, rust. With the introduction of the S2 Europa in time for the car's 1969 debut on the UK market, the design was changed to separate body and chassis like the Elan.

The export market was much in mind for the Europa (in France it was actually called Europe), and the first examples all went overseas. But, as it turned out, the Europa was later to lose its Renault engine because the French company didn't want to renew the deal. One of the reasons was pressure from Jean Redelé, whose Renault-powered, rear-engined Alpine sports car was the Europa's closest rival.

There's an interesting aside here. With France seen as a potentially strong market for the Europa, particularly if it remained Renault-powered, Chapman actually approached Redelé with the idea of his building the Europa under licence in France. It seemed a sensible notion but no deal was struck and, today, the V6-engined Renault Alpine (GTA in the UK) is arguably a closer rival to the Lotus Esprit than even a Ferrari 328 or a Porsche 911. Plastic body, backbone chassis, choice of normally aspirated or turbocharged rearward-mounted engine: the similarities are striking.

EUROPA GOES TWIN-CAM
. . . and fulfils its promise

Right from the start, Europas were built at Lotus's current factory at Hethel, near Norwich, to which the company moved during 1966. And, concurrently within the first batch of production cars, Lotus Components built some racing versions powered by Lotus's twin-cam engine and designated Lotus 47. With the Renault deal off, it was clear that roadgoing Europas would also end up similarly-powered – and one of the first tasks awaiting an ex-Jaguar engineer named Michael Kimberley, on his joining Lotus in 1969, was to re-engineer the Europa around this new engine.

Mike Kimberley, who is now chief executive and managing director of what has become Group Lotus, looked at more than just the engine. The fixed side windows were a major irritant, and those high side buttresses made three-quarter rear vision non-existent. So the Europa Twin-Cam, as it became known, found itself with electric windows and shallower buttresses over which the driver could see.

It also had an improved gear linkage (a Renault gearbox was retained, later with five speeds), and conventionally adjustable seats (previously, the seats were fixed and you adjusted the driving position by moving the pedals – a spanner job). Thus revised, this Lotus blossomed; it had the performance the original car lacked, the better to exploit a degree of grip and balance even the Elan could not match. The Europa had got off to a slow start, but a remarkable 9230 examples had been made by the time production petered out in 1975. By this time its spiritual successor, the Esprit, was almost ready to take its place in Lotus's New Order . . .

ELAN EXPANDS
New models, more speed

The Europa had forked off the Elan's evolutionary road, on a route which would lead ultimately to the Esprit, but meanwhile the Elan itself continued to develop. In 1966, the year of the move to Hethel, Lotus took over the machining work for the twin-cam cylinder heads from original contractors JAP; and during the following year JAP – by then taken over by Villiers – also relinquished the task of engine assembly which it had carried out since the Elan's launch. The same year, 1967, in which Lotus thus became an engine manufacturer also saw the introduction of the Elan S4, and the lengthened, restyled Elan Plus 2 which had space for two people in the back provided they were small.

Available only as a coupé, the Plus 2 was a move upmarket for Lotus and signalled the future direction Chapman desired for his company. Like all Lotuses of the time it could be bought in component form, but proportionately fewer Plus 2s were so supplied than were other Lotuses. This suited Colin Chapman fine; he was eager for Lotus to shed its kit-car, slightly home-made image and, instead, to see his cars judged on equal terms with the best that mainstream manufacturers could offer.

Indeed in 1969, the year after Lotus Cars became a public company, the Plus 2 ceased to be available as a kit. It also gained a 115bhp Plus 2S derivative. And the following year saw yet more power extracted from the twin-cam engine thanks to the work of ex-BRM engineer Tony Rudd (who is now Lotus's technical director). With larger valves, it now developed 126bhp. Fitted with the Big Valve engine, the Elan S4 was dubbed Sprint and sported a two-tone colour scheme inspired by the cigarette sponsor's colours used on the Formula 1 Lotus 49s, while the 126bhp Plus 2 became the Plus 2S 130 (having already dropped the Elan name).

Here, in the Sprint, was the ultimate Elan, the Elan most prized by enthusiasts today. Its performance was astonishing for the time: *Motor* magazine recorded a maximum speed of 121mph (194kph) and a standstill-to-60mph (97kph) time of just 6.7sec. Two years later, by which time Lotus's own five-speed gearbox was supplementing the Ford-based four-speed, the big-valve engine could be had in the Europa in which it travelled even faster.

The following year, 1973, saw the beginning of Value Added Tax (VAT) in Great Britain and the end of the Elan, with a total of 12,224 examples having been produced. These two events are linked, because VAT spelt the end of tax-free kit-car sales. Suddenly the Elan, hitherto sold mainly in component form, looked much too expensive; continued production, Lotus decided, was no longer viable.

Lotus's kit-car days were over. Within two years the Elan's offspring, the Europa and the Plus 2 (of which 5200 were made), would follow it into the history books. But Chapman didn't mind at all, for a new era was about to begin.

A NEW ENGINE
. . . and a new family of cars

A hint of what was to come had first been seen back in the late 1960s. This was the Lotus 904, or LV220, two-litre racing engine which used Lotus's own design of cylinder head. It boasted not only the obligatory twin overhead camshafts, but also four valves for each of its four cylinders. The cast-iron cylinder block of the 904 was a Vauxhall item – but it happened to be very close in its important dimensions to the aluminium block which Lotus was developing.

By 1971, under the direction of Tony Rudd, the block was ready and Lotus's first truly in-house engine could enter production. The 1973cc unit, designated 907, gave 140bhp on Dellorto carburettors and promptly found a home in the new Jensen-Healey sports car.

This arrangement brought in much-needed extra revenue, for Lotus was committed to an ambitious investment programme which would shortly see an entirely new range of upmarket, exclusive, larger engined cars bearing the proud Lotus emblem. The days of four-and-a-half thousand Lotuses leaving Hethel in a year, the all-time high reached in 1969, were to be banished

Below: The beginning of Lotus's New Order. The 2-litre 907 engine, of aluminium construction and featuring not only twin belt-driven overhead camshafts but also four valves per cylinder, put Lotus on the map as a true engine manufacturer. The first 907s, *developing 140bhp, were fitted to the ill-fated Jensen-Healey sports car from 1971, while Lotus developed its own range of upmarket, 907-powered cars for later in the decade. Current 900-series Lotus engines are basically similar, though there are many detail differences.*

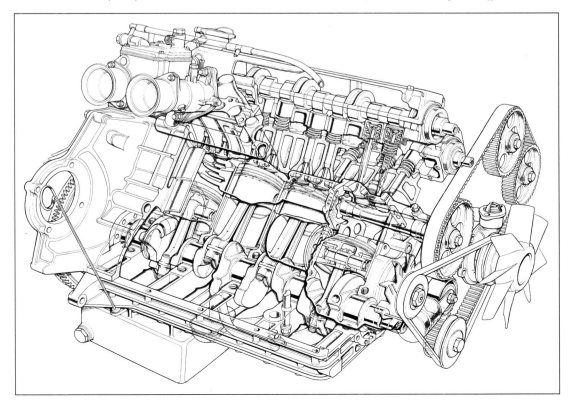

Left: The Eclat, introduced in 1975, was effectively a fastback Elite with a conventional boot instead of a hatchback. It turned out to be *more popular than its progenitor, and continues in production, although somewhat modified to become the Excel, to this day.*

for good; henceforth it was to be low volumes and high profit margins. Or so went the plan; two decades on, we are seeing Lotus about to enter once again the market it created, and then vacated, with the original Elan . . . though this time the new Elan will co-exist with more expensive Lotuses further up the range.

The first of the new generation Lotuses was Project M50, a car which resurrected the Elite name (and was also, in the mark number series, Lotus 75). The time taken to design a new car to comply with the ever-tightening noose of legislation, plus Britain's infamous three-day working week of the Winter of Discontent, caused the launch to be delayed until May 1974 – perfectly timed for the bottom to fall out of the luxury GT market following the oil crisis. But once it was launched, the Elite attracted much favourable comment. It was a striking car: its low, wedge-shaped body featured a waistline boldly upswept towards the rear, and at the tail was a Reliant Scimitar GTE-like hatchback.

Under the skin lay the familiar backbone chassis recipe, with Europa-like rear suspension, Lotus's own design of five-speed gearbox as used in the last Elans – it actually used Austin Maxi internals in a casing machined by Beans Industries, a one-time car maker by then under the British Leyland umbrella – and a Salisbury, instead of Ford, differential. After many years of relying on Ford for many proprietary parts, Lotus seemed finally to have severed the Ford connection. The body, styled by Lotus's own Oliver Winterbottom, was produced in separate top and bottom halves by Lotus's patented VARI (Vacuum Assisted Resin Injection) process; today's Lotus bodies are made the same way.

The first Elites were not the paragons of integrity their positioning in the marketplace demanded, for they were the victims of rushed, incomplete development in an effort to get them on sale and generate revenue. Their engines, uprated to 155bhp, were noisy, unrefined and lacking in low-speed pull; this, and flimsy interior fittings, disappointed the first buyers. But it wasn't all gloom: they found the roadholding and handling to be every bit as good as it should be in a Lotus, and the VARI bodywork to possess perhaps the finest finish then seen on a plastic-

Above: The first Lotus to receive the 907 engine was the new 1974 Elite. Styled by Oliver Winterbottom, it was bold in its day but looks *awkward now; its body pioneered the VARI process. With the Elite, which carried no Ford parts, Lotus severed the FoMoCo connection.*

bodied car. Within months, Lotus had the problems under control before the car developed a reputation like that of its earlier namesake, increasing the power (to 160bhp) and torque in the process. With the car thus honed, the outlook for the Elite's future began to brighten.

Right from the outset, Lotus had stressed that the Elite was the first of a family of three cars. The others would be a fastback four-seater with a boot, and a wedge-shaped mid-engined two-seater to carry on, further up the automotive social scale, where the Europa left off. All would be powered by the same engine and share common design themes. Come the 1975 Motor Show at Earl's Court, those two cars – the Eclat (M52) and the Esprit (M70) – duly appeared. The Eclat, an Elite with a more conventional tail, looked as people expected it to look; the Esprit, an angular wedge which threatened to scoop up anyone who got in its way, was a sensation. And with turbo-charging technology on the horizon, there would be plenty more of those.

11

COLIN CHAPMAN
The man who made Lotus

Anthony Colin Bruce Chapman – the initials form the Lotus logo – was born in Richmond, Surrey, England on 19 May 1928, the only son of Stan and Mary Chapman. He died, a millionaire, at 4am. 16 December 1982, after a heart attack. American Express was about to pull the financial plug on Lotus, and the scandal of the missing De Lorean millions was on the point of breaking. For Chapman, by then white-haired but thought fighting fit, it had all become too much. And the world lost the man who had become, during his fifty-four years, one of the most far-sighted car designers it had ever known.

During what were to be his last years, Chapman worked from Ketteringham Hall, the restored country house taken over as a think-tank and Team Lotus headquarters. The Hethel operation, he thought, could look after itself; deep down, Colin Chapman had never really wanted to be a car manufacturer. That was merely a means to support his first love, motor racing. As Lotus's status as a car manufacturer grew, he became ever more willing to distance himself from it.

The racing side of Lotus, in fact, was hived off as a separate company as early as 1953, for tax reasons. Yet for many years hence, the car-making side would be expected to contribute large sums to what had, by the late 1950s, become Team Lotus. Not that the manufacturing side could complain; the publicity for the Lotus name accruing from six Formula One World Drivers' Championships, and seven World Constructors' Championships, helped the road car business immeasurably.

Chapman – sometimes mercurial, always innovative, often impatient, crushingly logical, 100 per cent his own boss – is remembered as an engineering genius, able to inspire those who worked with him to devastating effect. You can see why. His clear, analytical mind fostered an engineering approach in which nothing was taken for granted; he always started from first principles, from a fresh, detached viewpoint. This approach became Lotus's trademark, and those same principles hold true in Lotus activities today.

Simplicity, rigidity and lightness were Chapman's goals in his cars, but brute force and crudity were out. Perhaps his early training as a structural engineer pointed him in this direction, for even the very first Lotus – his 1948 Austin Seven-based trials car with its stressed aluminium/plywood skin – showed the way his mind would later work.

FORMULA ONE LOTUSES
Fruits of a fertile brain

Just a few examples serve to show the depth of Chapman's influence on the world in which his heart lay, Formula One motor racing. He pioneered adjustable, 'tunable' suspension systems. He introduced the monocoque chassis with its aviation-style bag fuel tanks; the Lotus 25 so-designed helped Jim Clark to his 1963 World Championship win, repeated in 1965 with the Lotus 33. (Earlier, the original Elite had been the first glassfibre monocoque road car.) He introduced the aerodynamic wedge shape, on the 1968

Above: Colin Chapman, the mercurial genius whose mind made Lotus great. A fervent non-smoker, he had the inside *window sills of the restored Ketteringham Hall made with a slope to prevent people from putting ashtrays on them.*

gas-turbine Lotus 56 Indianapolis car; following that, he was the first to fit aerodynamic wings to a Formula One car (although it had already been tried in sports car racing, notably by Chaparral). Graham Hill, in a Lotus 49 so-equipped, won the 1968 World Drivers' Championship.

The Lotus 72 of 1970 was the instigator of the present-day F1 look, with its wedge nose and side-mounted radiators. Two more championships came Lotus's way that year, the drivers' one going – posthumously, owing to his fatal accident at Monza – to Jochen Rindt. Two years later Emerson Fittipaldi was champion, in a 72 again. The year after, 1973, saw the Lotus 72 win the Constructors' Championship yet again, but this time – the only time it happened – without a Lotus driver winning the Drivers' Championship.

It was 1978 before these glories were repeated, the year in which the Lotus 79 ground-effect racer, developed from the 78 wing car, won the double championship crown with Mario Andretti becoming the World Champion driver. As had happened time and again before, a new Chapman concept had swept all before it and everyone else had to copy. It was to be Lotus's last Championship win to date.

Sometimes, though, Chapman's revolutionary designs were banned instead. The one that caused the greatest acrimony, that tried Chapman's commitment to the very limit, was the twin-chassis concept used in the Lotus 86 and 88 of 1980–81. This concept was of potentially devastating effectiveness, as it made the best possible use of aerodynamic downforce without subjecting the driver to the back-breaking ride hardness inherent in the minute suspension travel of a ground-effect car with side skirts. After numerous legal battles, it was decreed that the second chassis (that which supported

the ground-effect bodywork) was a movable aerodynamic device and therefore not allowed. Neither car ever raced.

FLUCTUATING FORTUNES
Chapman's vision pulls Lotus through

All this, of course, must be overlaid on the possibly less glamorous, but ultimately more important, activities of what has become Group Lotus – that is to say, everything Lotus bar the Formula One racing team.

With the Elan, and later the Europa, selling well in the 1960s, and the company safely installed at Hethel with plenty of room to expand, the outlook was good. Lotus had become a public company in October 1968, with shares floated on the Stock Exchange, followed by a record year in 1969, with 4506 cars produced and profits to match. After that, though, production began to slide as the buying public began to tire of what was becoming an ageing model range.

This was not mirrored in the Group's profits, however, because the deal to build engines for the Jensen-Healey sports car was a lucrative one – lucrative enough to finance the development of the second-generation Elite. But the oil crisis of 1973–4 plunged Lotus into a crisis of its own: with the upmarket new Elite imminent, suddenly no one wanted upmarket GT cars. Yet here was Lotus about to be, briefly, a one-model company as the Elan/Europa family faded out.

Profits tumbled in 1974, and 1975 saw a loss of nearly £½m with excessively high pricing and poor demand for the Elite taking their toll. But Chapman did not lose his nerve. He knew that the only way out of the mess was to continue to invest in the future, in the Eclat and – especially – the Esprit. This is why these two new cars were shown together at the 1975 Earl's Court motor show, even though it would be months before Lotus could afford to put the Esprit – vital to the once-thriving US market – into production.

Total Lotus production in 1975 was a disastrous 535 cars, but 1976 saw this figure nearly doubled and the company slip back into a marginal profit. This was despite the demise of Jensen Motors and the termination of the engine deal which had been worth, at best, 4000 engines a year, and was a direct result of the success of the Esprit even though the start of production had been delayed until June.

This was also the year in which Colin Chapman moved his office permanently to Ketteringham Hall, away from the aggravation of running the Hethel car factory, a job he was happy to leave to Mike Kimberley. There, Chapman could concentrate on designs for racing cars, Moonraker boats (also made by the VARI process, which he invented), and, later, microlight aircraft (flying was a passion second only to racing). He could also get on with running Team Lotus.

It is said that his heart was no longer in the road car business, and indeed it hadn't been since Group Lotus had gone public. The stock market flotation, although lucrative for Chapman in the short term (it made him a millionaire), left him feeling that he was no longer in full control and that didn't suit him at all. The Esprit was to be the last Lotus road car with which Chapman was involved.

SURVIVAL BY DIVERSIFICATION
Enter American Express
Come 1977, things were picking up and profits were healthier. But it was clear that the company needed to broaden its base if it was to survive, so Chapman set up an engineering consultancy which, he hoped, other manufacturers would use when they needed specific development work done. And, to finance expansion plans, a £2.6 million loan and overdraft facility repayable over five years was agreed with American Express.

The consultancy soon had plenty of work to do, for at the end of 1978 it took on the task of redesigning John Zachary De Lorean's rear-engined sports coupé and making it a viable production proposition. It was a lucrative contract, completed against mounting odds in a record twenty-five months; yet the striking stainless-steel-clad coupé with its gullwing doors, made near Belfast but designed for the US, was a flop. It was too slow, its handling was suspect despite Lotus having made the very best of a bad job, and it cost too much.

The De Lorean enterprise folded in 1982, having cost the UK government millions of pounds in subsidies and grants for setting up the factory in employment starved Northern Ireland, and it was not long before the can of worms was opened. High finance, suspected drugs deals . . . the De Lorean scandal was a big one. What Colin Chapman's involvement was with the money that went missing, if indeed there was any at all, we shall probably never know. A crisis usually brought out the best in Chapman, but there were those who said that this time he had sailed too close to the wind.

During 1979, Lotus also adapted the Talbot Sunbeam to take the 911 engine and a ZF gearbox, in a deal similar to the 1963 one which had resulted in the Lotus Cortina. Final assembly of the Talbot Sunbeam Lotus was at Hethel, and this extremely rapid car was unashamedly a homologation special to enable Talbot to go rallying. This it did, with considerable success, and 2298 examples had been made by the end of production in 1981.

THE BRINK BECKONS
Crisis – and tragedy
That year, 1981, was the nadir of Lotus's road car operation. Distribution problems had wiped out sales in the important US market, and the recession triggered by the second oil crisis helped to depress 1981's Lotus production to just 345 cars. Trading figures showed a loss of £109,000 that year, compared with a £1.3 million profit two years earlier and the first loss since 1975. Worse, Lotus had been forced to borrow a further £250,000 just to service the interest on American Express's loan.

Things were looking bad – but the tenacious Chapman (who still retained control of Group Lotus's long-term strategy) reacted in his usual, positive way. The prices of the cars were cut dramatically to stimulate de-

mand, the loyal workforce was pared to the bone despite the pain this caused, and a co-operation agreement was signed with Toyota which meant that Lotus could use Toyota's reliable components to the benefit of Lotus quality. In return, Toyota could call on Lotus expertise. The brilliant Toyota MR2 mid-engined sports car may have been a fruit of this agreement, though no one has admitted it.

On the Lotus side, a Toyota engine was planned for the new, high-volume M90 sports car designed to take Lotus back into the affordable sports car sector. The company had realised that the decision to abandon the Elan market had, in retrospect, not been the right one, and plans were afoot for the M90 to take Lotus production levels back up to the 4–5000 a year level of the late 1960s, In the meantime, the Eclat was revised as the Excel with many Toyota components.

The Excel was launched at the October 1982 Paris and UK motor shows, to highly favourable reviews. Orders poured in, and things were looking up; the only problem was that American Express, concerned that Lotus had thus far paid back just £900,000 of the £2.6 million loan by the deal's September 1982 expiry date, was threatening to pull

out. Lotus, heading again for a trading loss in 1982, needed to find a new backer, and fast, if it was going to survive at all – never mind invest for the M90.

Meanwhile, Chapman's first love, Team Lotus, was in the doldrums having failed to win a single race in 1979, 1980 and 1981 and only one in 1982. The blind alley of the twin-chassis Lotus 88 had proved a heavy financial drain, at a time when Group Lotus could least afford to subsidise the racing team. For Colin Chapman, hardly anything seemed to be going right. There was pressure from all sides.

At 5am, on the morning of 16 December, just a few hours after Chapman had landed in his aeroplane at Hethel airfield having returned from a meeting with the motor sport ruling body in Paris, Hazel Chapman telephoned Lotus financial director Fred Bushell to say that her husband had suffered a massive heart attack. Colin Chapman, a man who dismissed the past and for whom the future could never come quickly enough, was dead.

Below: Jim Clark and Colin Chapman had a very special relationship, one which Chapman could never repeat with any other Lotus Formula One driver. Clark's death at Hockenheim in 1968, in a Formula Two Lotus 48 like the one he is driving here, affected Chapman deeply.

THE ORIGINAL ESPRIT

From Giorgetto Giugiaro's styling study, through mid-engined production car, to turbocharged supercar

W E HAVE SEEN how the Esprit, the mid-engined, wedge-shaped two-seater designed to take over from the Europa and complete Lotus's all-new range, made its debut at the 1975 Earl's Court Motor Show. But we were given a clue to the car's form well before then – on the Ital Design stand at the 1972 Turin Show. Here, Giorgetto Giugiaro, one of the founders of the Ital Design styling house on the outskirts of Turin, showed a smooth, striking, wedge-shaped, silver coupé with two seats and an engine behind them. Beneath the angular, sharp-edged bodywork lay a cut and stretched Europa chassis: here was a concept car to show how the Esprit would look, two years before even the Elite was ready for production.

GIORGETTO GIUGIARO
A chance meeting sows the seed

Tony Rudd had been busy with the new 16-valve engines since his arrival from BRM in 1969, but during 1970 he found time to stand back and draft the first proposals for Lotus's new range. Those for the front-engined cars (Elite and Eclat) were speedily put into action, but although the proposal for what was to become the Esprit gained board approval by the end of the year, that project found itself on the back burner while efforts were concentrated on what were expected to be the higher-volume cars.

There it might have stayed, had Giugiaro not approached Colin Chapman and Mike Kimberley at the 1971 Geneva Motor Show and asked if he could create a styling exercise using a Lotus as a base. Chapman, flattered by this recognition of Lotus as a company fit to be associated with a fast-blossoming Italian styling house, and mindful of the nascent M70 (Esprit) project, suggested a Europa chassis – and thus was the Esprit, at that stage still unnamed, conceived.

Giugiaro was no stranger to the styling of exotic cars. While working for Bertone in the early 1960s, he styled cars like the Alfa Romeo

2600 Sprint and the Giulia GT (later to become the original GTV), plus the Iso Grifo, Fiat Dino Coupé and Fiat 850 Spider; then, at Ghia, he was responsible for the Maserati Ghibli and the De Tomaso Mangusta. Ital Design, formed with Giugiaro's present partner Aldo Mantovani, was set up in 1968; as well as the Esprit, its work has included the Maserati Bora and Merak, the Alfasud and its Sprint coupé derivative, the original VW Passat and Audi 80, the original VW Golf and Scirocco, the DeLorean DMC-12, the Fiat Panda and Uno, the Isuzu Piazza, the BMW M1, the Saab 9000/Lancia Thema/Fiat Croma Type Four cars, the Renault 21 and many, many more. Giugiaro is one of the most prolific designers in the world, perhaps *the* most prolific.

GIUGIARO GETS TO WORK
'The Silver Car' is born

Lotus had envisaged the M70 as having a 98in. (2489mm) wheelbase. That of the Europa was much shorter, at just 91in. (2311mm), so before the chassis could be shipped to Ital Design it needed to be cut in half for an extra section to be welded in. It needed a wider track, too, as the M70 was to be a wider car and considerably roomier than the claustrophobic Europa.

Giugiaro's concept cars have invariably been finished in silver, and the Lotus was no exception. It was only logical, then, that Lotus should dub it 'The Silver Car' before the Esprit name was finalised. A wedge shape Lotus had wanted, and a wedge shape it most certainly got – all angles and flat, tautly skinned panels. This was Giugiaro's 'folded paper' period; the central depression in the front bonnet panel was another of his contemporary trade marks. Just look at an Alfasud or a Mark 1 Golf.

In detail it differed from the car's eventual production form, notably by having bonnet louvres, a curved windscreen and a fully-opening rear body section like that of, say, a Ford GT40 or a Ferrari F40, but the basic design was right on the

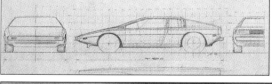

Below: Giugiaro's concept sketches and renderings show how the Esprit shape started as a Maserati-like profile, then developed into the characteristic Esprit style *with steeply raked windscreen pillars and a near-square rear side window. The 1972 Turin Show car, all lines and edges, was almost exactly as the main rendering here.*

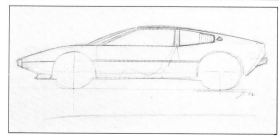

mark. Inside, too, the die had been cast; in front of the driver was a boomerang-shaped instrument and switchgear binnacle atop a low shelf, a design which remains part of the Esprit concept to this day. Beneath the huge rear window lay the Lotus 907 engine – but no gearbox, as a suitable unit had yet to be found.

First shown at the 1972 Turin Show, this non-running prototype was a huge hit. Much encouraged by this, and mindful that exotic mid-engined sports coupés were notably successful in the lucrative US market, Lotus decided to put the car into production. But there was a great deal of detail work to be done first.

FROM CONCEPT TO PRODUCTION REALITY
'The Red Car'

Wind tunnel testing showed up problems with aerodynamic lift, which would involve subtle modifications to the tail and chin spoiler under the front bumper. But, more fundamentally, the body as designed couldn't have been removed from a glassfibre mould. A further problem concerned the windscreen, raked back so that it was just 22° from the horizontal which it was thought might contravene visibility legislation.

Giancarlo Perini, now Italian correspondent for *Car* magazine, was involved with Ital Design at the time, and he organised for Mike Kimberley and Oliver Winterbottom (the Lotus designer who styled the 1974 Elite) to stay in Turin at his mother's flat. This they did, off and on, for a year, to work with Giugiaro on a second full-size styling model built on a development chassis close to the final production article. Colin Chapman, meanwhile, flew out to Turin up to three times a week in his own aeroplane to direct the project, sometimes with his Lotus colleagues also aboard if they weren't already there.

Winterbottom had to ensure that the bodyshell could be manufactured, like the Elite's, in separate top and bottom halves. This was simply achieved by accentuating the feature line around the car's midriff, to form the point at which the two mouldings would join. The idea was to produce Esprit bodies by the VARI process used

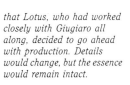

Below: The 1972 Ital Design concept car, known as 'The Silver Car' and based on a stretched Europa chassis, caused a sensation at the Turin Show – so much so, *that Lotus, who had worked closely with Giugiaro all along, decided to go ahead with production. Details would change, but the essence would remain intact.*

for the Elite, but in practice this never happened and Esprit bodies were hand-laid right up to the launch of the redesigned car in 1987.

The other main problem was that windscreen rake, given that neither Giugiaro nor Chapman wanted to spoil the forward-thrusting shape of the A-pillar. The solution came, as moments of genius often do, at around 2am in the morning. Kimberley recalls how he, Chapman, Giugiaro and Winterbottom were covered in white plaster, trying to sculpt that A-pillar until it looked right, but failing. Chapman, innovative as ever, was the one who solved the problem – leave the pillars as they were, and move the centre line of the windscreen (which was originally shaped as though a section from a cone) back until the screen was virtually flat, and sloping at the same 26° angle as the pillars.

The first prototype, painted red and consequently named 'The Red Car', was brought back to Lotus in 1973, and taken to Ketteringham Hall, not far from the Hethel factory, where the project continued under the leadership of Colin Spooner (now Director of Design). This retreat, now the headquarters of Team Lotus and no longer connected with Group Lotus Ltd, was used at that time as a secluded think-tank as well as a base for the works racing team.

Above: Now fifty years old, Giorgio Giugiaro (he is more commonly known by the diminutive form, Giorgetto) is arguably the world's greatest *car stylist, and also the most prolific. The only one who comes close is the man who took his place at Bertone, Marcello Gandini.*

A RUNNING PROTOTYPE
And a search for a gearbox

The Europa's five-speed Renault transaxle wasn't strong enough to cope with the outputs of the 2-litre Lotus engine, never mind the more potent power plants already in the minds of Chapman, Kimberley, Rudd *et al.*, and Lotus couldn't afford to make its own, so an alternative had to found. Clearly, the Elite gearbox was unsuitable as it was designed for a front-engine, rear-wheel-drive car; that for the M70 needed to be a two-shaft unit with an integral differential.

Citroën provided the answer, in the form of the transaxle used in the front of the Citroën-Maserati SM and the rear of the mid-engined Maserati Merak (the French company owned Maserati at the time). Even the ratios were right, and Citroën was prepared to guarantee supply for many years.

Time was tight, for the Europa's days were numbered; Lotus badly needed the income that US sales would produce. A running prototype by the end of 1974 was the aim, with production and the public launch the following year.

Development proceeded apace, along predictable lines. As with the Elite, the engine was canted over at 45° to the left and would be offered in 160bhp tune. That the engine bay might later house a Lotus V8 was an enticing possibility, still not realised . . . though it could just happen, as we'll see later. Rear suspension, too, was like the Elite's, with both transverse and semi-trailing lower links to act like a wide-based wishbone, and the drive shaft doubling as an upper suspension arm. As ever with a Lotus, springing was by combined coil spring/damper units front and rear; front suspension, though still a double wishbone layout, used Opel Ascona components instead of the Triumph-inspired items of the Elite. The all-disc brakes were by Alfred Teves (Ate) on the prototype; production cars would use Girling equipment.

At this stage, Colin Chapman decided to chop 2in. (51mm) out of the wheelbase, to end up at 96in. (244mm). It was done for aesthetic reasons: Mike Kimberley recalls that he fought against the change, and lost. It meant that drivers as tall

as the lanky Kimberley would never fit satisfactorily in the Esprit, as the 2in. came out of the passenger compartment, but the shorter Chapman didn't see this as a problem. Chapman, too, had a long back which is why the Esprit's steering wheel was mounted so high. The first Esprits didn't have reclining seats, either, so the only way to be truly comfortable was to be of the same height and proportions as Chapman.

PREMATURE BIRTH
Paris Show sensation

The prototype was, indeed, running by the end of 1974 (Christmas Eve, in fact), and by then the name had been finalised. Giugiaro wanted to call the car Kiwi, on account of its long, pointed nose, but this was thought not to suit the English-speaking and shoe-polishing world – and besides, the car's name had to begin with 'E'.

But it was to be a long time before the Esprit was ready for production. A myriad detail problems had still to be overcome, and when a pre-production car was shown at the Paris Motor Show in October 1975, and Britain's Earl's Court Show later that month with the new Eclat, it was still some way from going on sale. But at least the public was able, at last, to see the Esprit for itself.

With its fat Wolfrace wheels, low, unusually wide stance and dramatic styling, the silver Esprit made an impressive sight. It seemed fine value, too, at £5844 – notably cheaper than the Elite. However, Lotus's parlous financial state meant that money was tight for final development, and in the event the Esprit didn't enter production until May 1976. By the time the first examples were sold, the price had climbed dramatically to a worryingly high £7883.

These first Esprits, retrospectively known as S1, had self-coloured bodywork. This innovation certainly saved labour at the factory, but the snag was the limited number of colours available. Metallic finishes, often specified by buyers of

Above: The S1 of 1975, the first production Esprit, was little changed from the 'Red Car'. The wheelbase was 2in. (51mm) shorter, the fuel filler was redesigned, and the centre side pillars were finished in black. The first cars had self-coloured bodywork.

expensive machinery, were incompatible with the process, and before long Lotus reverted to conventional spray painting. (Now, in the late 1980s, the process may return in a modified form.)

The car gained mixed reviews from the motoring press, once they had been able to drive it. Of the excellence of the roadholding and handling there were no doubts; but of the steering feel, visibility, refinement and build quality there were plenty. Nor were the cars as fast as expected, failing to reach 130mph (209kph) when Lotus claimed 138 (222kph). However, this did not deter Lotus's United States importer from pressing ahead with plans to sell the Esprit, suitably re-engineered for US emissions and safety legislation, in North America. Launched there in 1977, it sold like hot pretzels until the distribution arrangement fell apart. In 1989, Lotus's US presence is once again strong thanks to the import organisation now being wholly under the control of Lotus.

DETAIL DEVELOPMENT
Esprit S2 and S2.2

'Detail' is right, for the S2 of August 1978 showed no radical changes. In essence, the changes consisted of an integrated wrap-around nose spoiler instead of a tacked-on blade, discreet air scoops behind the rear side windows to aid cooling, improved instrumentation, seats and trim, and four-spoke Speedline wheels in place of the Wolfrace 'Slot Mags'. The S2 also had the 'E' camshafts introduced in all Lotuses during 1977, with a revised profile to improve both mid-range pulling power and exhaust cleanliness, and subtle changes to the front wheel offset, damper settings and steering column bearings – this last to reduce 'stiction'.

There was no doubt that the S2 was a better car than its predecessor, more comfortable and more confidence-inspiring, but performance, though undeniably strong, still fell short of expectations. *Motor* magazine's car achieved over 130mph (209kph) and accelerated from a standstill to 60mph (97kph) in 7.7sec, but Lotus reckoned the latter figure should have been 6.8sec. More importantly, the wind roar and body booms were as bad as they had ever been; using

Below: The first Esprit suffered from many shortcomings, particularly lack of refinement and patchy build quality. Things improved with the S2, and again with the S2.2 of 1980, pictured here, which had the enlarged, 2.2-litre, 912 engine. The S2.2 is the rarest Esprit, only 88 being made before the S3 replaced it.

the driveshaft as an upper suspension link meant that the engine/transaxle unit had to be mounted almost rigidly in the chassis in order to maintain correct suspension geometry during cornering, and this meant that a lot of noise was fed into the car's structure. The Lotus Esprit, it seemed, had some way to go before it could match the polish of a Porsche, or even a Ferrari.

At the beginning of 1980, the faithful 907 engine was replaced by a longer-stroke unit with a capacity raised from 1973cc to 2174cc (120.3–132.7 cu.in.). Known as the 912, this engine produced no more power but an extra 20lb ft of torque, bringing the latter's total to 160lb ft at 5000rpm. Only eighty-eight examples of the resulting Esprit S2.2 were built between January 1980 and March 1981 when it was replaced by the vastly improved S3, a car which was to bear the fruits of development originally carried out for an altogether higher purpose. Yes, exciting things had been happening to the Esprit. . .

ENTER THE TURBO
Aspirations heightened
Here is where the story of Esprit, the fully-fledged supercar, begins. Launched in February 1980, the last-minute guest at a lavish party held at London's Royal Albert Hall and hosted by Team Lotus sponsor Essex Petroleum, project M72 – the 210bhp, 2.2-litre, 152mph (244kph) Turbo Esprit, resplendent in its Essex colours of blue, red and silver – was just the boost Lotus needed.

At that moment only three cars existed, so launching the Turbo Esprit at Essex's party, originally intended to spread the word about the

Above: It was gains all round with the S3. Not only did it have the stronger chassis of the Turbo, with its greatly improved rear suspension which no longer used the

driveshaft as a noise-transmitting upper link, but it was actually cheaper than the S2.2 it replaced. Lotus hoped the price cut would revive flagging sales; it did.

Below: The Turbo Esprit, launched in 1980, secured Lotus's entry into the supercar league. Its looks gave ample warning of intent, with black extractor louvres

on the rear deck and purposeful air scoops in the flared sills. This is a late example, with body-colour bumpers; earlier Esprits had black bumpers.

mysterious petrol company's motor sport involvement, was something of a publicity stunt.
Those three cars afterwards went to Colin Chapman, Essex chief David Thieme, and an unnamed
managing director of one of Lotus's components
suppliers. The public wouldn't be able to buy
until August.

But the Turbo Esprit – these words weren't
reversed until the current car was launched in
1987 – was much more than just a Lotus Esprit
with a Garrett T3 turbocharger attached. Without
changing the basic body, Giorgetto Giugiaro had
added lashings of visual muscle: a deep, wraparound front air dam led visually into equally
deep, outward-flared sills incorporating NACA
ducts at their rear ends for exhaust cooling. This
lower, meatier body line continued around the
back in an under-bumper valance through which
projected the twin exhaust pipes.

In place of the huge, sloping rear window
were stepped slats in black, the uppermost one of
which bore a lip to direct the airflow away from
the lower slats, and thus create a low-pressure
area to help extract warm air from the engine
compartment. A vertical rear window, immediately behind the passenger compartment, of
course remained. Remarkably, the drag coefficient was claimed barely to be altered (the truth
is somewhat different) and, indeed, the balance
of aerodynamic forces on front and rear axles was
actually closer to being equal.

Spoke-pattern wheels, initially by Compomo-
tive but later changed to BBS, were shod with
even fatter Goodyear NCT tyres: 195/60 VR15 on
the front, 235/60 VR15 on the back, maintaining
the front/rear size differential the Esprit had
always shown. A pronounced lip spoiler on the
car's tail completed the visual transformation.

Cynics would say that the purity of the original
Esprit had been swamped, with the car now
looking like a collection of add-on parts, but there
was no denying its purposeful aggression.

NEW SUSPENSION
And a strengthened chassis
The new look was more than just skin deep, for
underneath was a thoroughly redesigned chassis
to cope with 152mph and acceleration to match.
Gone, at last, was the use of the driveshaft as the
rear suspension's top link; in its place was a
separate transverse link, and the driveshaft
gained a plunging constant-velocity joint so it
could move within the new geometry. This meant
that the engine could sit on absorbent, four-point
mountings to the great benefit of refinement, and
it took a lot of the stresses out of the wheel and
transaxle bearings.

At the front, too, the suspension had changed.
In place of the Opel-derived parts, there was the
Lotus-made upper wishbone/lower transverse
link system by then already in use on the front-
engined cars. These new suspension systems
were hung on to a greatly strengthened galvanised backbone chassis, with triangulation reinforcement at stress points and boxing-in of previously open sections. And, intriguingly, the
tubular engine cradle was wider . . . to take a V8?
Speculation was rife, because it was known that
prototype 4-litre V8 Esprits with 330bhp – project M71 – had been running.

Front brake discs went up in diameter from
9.7in. (246mm) to 10.5in. (266mm), and were
thicker too, but still not ventilated. Nor were the
rear discs; these were still located inboard next
to the Citroën transaxle, itself unchanged despite
its maker's fears that it would be unable to cope

*Above: Inside the Turbo
Esprit, the feel was much as
in Giugiaro's original concept
with its striking 'boomerang'
instrument panel. The leather*
*upholstery, though
sumptuous, was apt to look
overblown. Note the high
position of the steering wheel,
and the backbone tunnel.*

with 200lb ft of turbo torque. At least the clutch
was bigger.

BLOWING HARD
Turbocharged transformation
The heart of the Turbo Esprit, of course, was its
engine. Although similar, superficially, to other
Lotus 900-series engines, the 910 Turbo engine
was comprehensively re-engineered for its new,
highly-stressed rôle. New pistons, with their
crowns and piston rings lowered relative to the
gudgeon pin, reduced the compression ratio from
9.4:1 to 7.5:1 to avoid detonation when the
engine was running at high turbo boost levels,
and revised camshafts both opened the sixteen
valves further and kept them open longer. This
was unusual; in general, turbocharged engines
have *less* valve-opening duration than the equivalent normally aspirated unit. The exhaust valves
were sodium-filled in the interests of better heat
transfer.

Instead of five separate main bearing caps, the
Lotus engine uses an integrated main bearing
panel: this was strengthened. A larger radiator
was fed by a higher-capacity water pump, and the
water passages in the cylinder head were enlarged. There was slight overkill in the lubrication system, this using a dry sump and a separate
oil tank – plus, of course, an additional pump to
scavenge oil from the bottom of the engine and
return it to the tank. This mirrored racing practice, and was adopted to overcome problems with
oil surge during fast cornering, and to ensure a

big enough oil capacity to prevent the engine running low during a long, fast run. Needless to say, there was an oil cooler too.

In March 1983, the Turbo Esprit reverted to a conventional wet-sump system, fitted with radial sump baffles as developed for the V8 to cure oil surge and consequent starvation of the lubrication system during hard cornering. Tony Rudd remembers that the radial baffles even coped with the development Esprit fitted with Lotus's springless Active Suspension system, which generated higher cornering forces than he had ever seen in a road car.

All this was to ensure that the engine could cope with the extra output that the American Garrett AiResearch T3 turbocharger, blowing through the Dellorto 40 DHLA twin-venturi side-draught carburettors, could liberate. This was the first time that these carburettors had been used on the pressurised side of a forced-induction system, so they incorporated pressure seals around the throttle spindles to stop the pressurised petrol/air mix from escaping. The Lotus system remains unusual among turbocharged, carburettor-fed engines in blowing, rather than sucking, through the carburettors.

FORCED INDUCTION
How the turbocharger works

The turbocharger was – and is – mounted in a specially made exhaust manifold, originally of silicon–molybdenum iron but now made of stainless steel, and able to resist the red heat at which it and the turbocharger would run under load. Exhaust gases spin a turbine wheel at speeds of up to 110,000rpm, and that wheel is connected by a shaft to another positioned just downstream of the air filter. This second turbine wheel compresses the incoming air at a pressure of up to 0.55bar (8psi) before the air enters the

carburettor venturis and thence the engine.

By compressing the air, a greater quantity of it can be mixed with petrol and forced into the cylinders than would be possible by relying on cylinder suction alone – so when the mixture fires, there's a bigger bang and more power. There is a limit to how far you can go, though, both in terms of engine strength and because the more you compress air, the hotter it gets. If it gets too hot, the engine will suffer pre-ignition ('pinking') and pistons will melt. So this doesn't happen, there is a safety valve, or wastegate, which causes the exhaust side of the turbo-

Above: Schematic diagram of the turbocharger installation. In practice the turbocharger is installed behind the engine, rather than on top as the diagram suggests. The

wastegate as shown here is separate from the turbocharger, linked to the inlet side of it by a pressure pipe. Arrow in turbocharger shows rotation of shaft.

charger to be by-passed, preventing a further build-up of boost, when the inlet tract pressure exceeds 0.55bar.

There's a further complication. So that fuel doesn't get forced out of the carburettor float chambers by the boost pressure, they are sealed and the fuel supply from the two petrol tanks,

INSTALLATION OF TURBOCHARGER

Turbocharger

Exhaust

Plenum chamber

Carburettor

→ Air

→ Compressed air

→ Compressed air/fuel mixture

→ Exhaust gas

→ Bypass exhaust gas

Wastegate

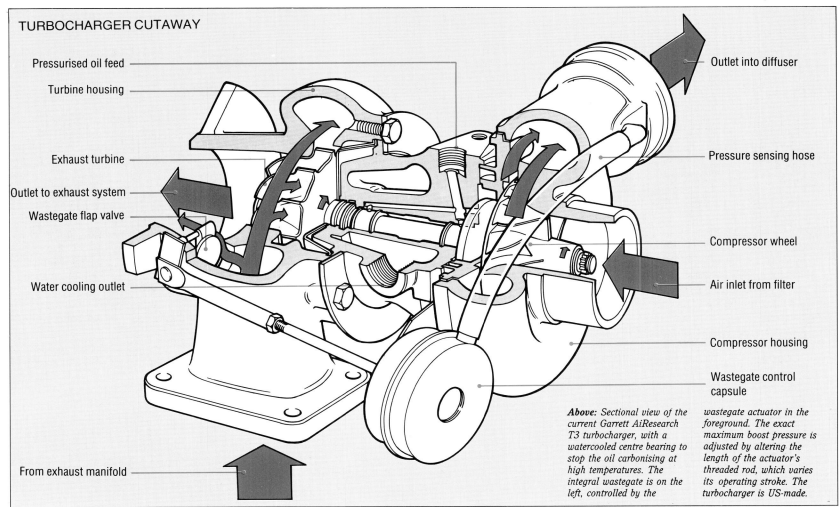

TURBOCHARGER CUTAWAY

Pressurised oil feed

Turbine housing

Exhaust turbine

Outlet to exhaust system

Wastegate flap valve

Water cooling outlet

From exhaust manifold

Outlet into diffuser

Pressure sensing hose

Compressor wheel

Air inlet from filter

Compressor housing

Wastegate control capsule

Above: Sectional view of the current Garrett AiResearch T3 turbocharger, with a watercooled centre bearing to stop the oil carbonising at high temperatures. The integral wastegate is on the left, controlled by the

wastegate actuator in the foreground. The exact maximum boost pressure is adjusted by altering the length of the actuator's threaded rod, which varies its operating stroke. The turbocharger is US-made.

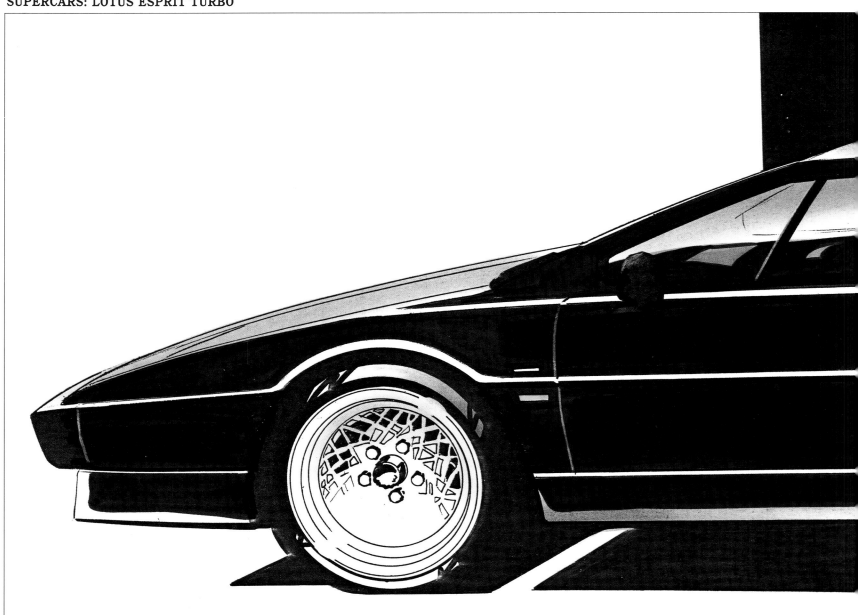

normally pressurised by the pump at 0.3bar (4.5psi), is increased in pressure by an amount corresponding to the boost at a given instant. This is achieved by a pressure regulating valve, operated by a spring-loaded diaphragm which moves according to turbo boost pressure.

NO INTERCOOLER
But a better throttle response
Some turbocharged engines have intercoolers – a heat exchanger, typically resembling a radiator, through which the compressed air passes before being fed into the inlet tract. The idea is to lower the air temperature, which means the engine can run at a higher boost pressure, and thus compress the air more, without the air getting hot enough to cause damage. Lotus decided against this for two reasons. It would have meant a longer path from turbocharger to inlet tract, and thus more lag (the delay between the turbine wheels spinning and the engine making use of the boost pressure) and there was nowhere to put a bulky intercooler anyway!

In fact, the plenum chamber between turbocharger and carburettors is finned, which gives some cooling effect. And there's an advantage to

Right: *Since the introduction of the turbo, all Esprits have used this extra-strong version of the typically Lotus backbone frame. It is fabricated from steel sheet and tube, and then galvanised; the tubular engine cradle is wide enough to take a V8. Points 1 to 12 indicate where chassis will be fixed to body of car.*

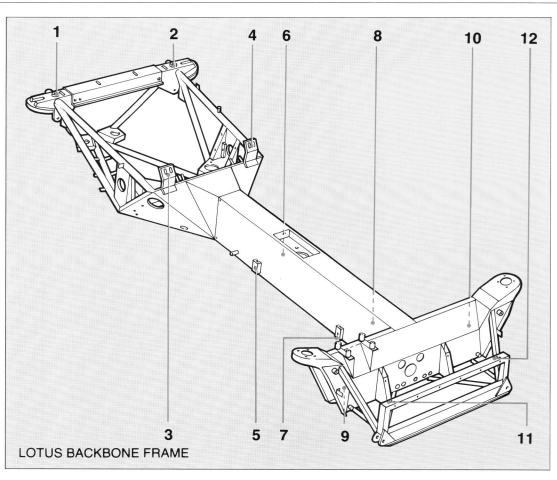

LOTUS BACKBONE FRAME

the Lotus approach – the short path from turbo to cylinder, and the unusual (for a turbo) down-stream position of the carburettors right next to the inlet tract, gives the turbocharged Esprit a crispness and immediacy of throttle response that makers of other turbocharged cars only dream about. Not that Lotus eschews intercool-ers on principle; as we shall see, there are ways around the problems . . .

ESSEX TURBO
Small numbers, high price

The £20,950 asking price for the original, multi-coloured Essex Turbo Esprit was a phenomenal amount of money by the standards of 1980. A highly complicated, roof-mounted National Panasonic sound system was part of the reason, as were ruched leather seats and air condition-ing. After 104 Essex-liveried cars had been built, Lotus switched in April 1981 to conventional colours which pleased the less exhibitionist cus-tomers. Leather and air conditioning became options and the sound system was discontinued; it had been FM-only, which in 1980 was not appreciated by customers.

Thus rationalised, the Turbo Esprit dropped dramatically in price to £16,917 and sales shot up correspondingly. In 1982 the car became Lotus's biggest selling model – and that was without tapping the lucrative US market, from which Lotus had retired, hurt, after further pro-blems with distributors. The Esprit S3, too, was

selling strongly; a far better car than the short-lived S2.2, and cheaper too at £13,461, it had the Turbo's improved chassis and some of its styling updates. Things were looking up for Lotus, for the Turbo Esprit was destined to be a major Stateside success.

EVOLUTION INTO REVOLUTION
Esprit comes of age

From shaky beginnings, the Lotus Esprit had developed into a true supercar. The Turbo was very fast: *Motor* tested one and achieved a 0–60mph (0–97kph) time of 5.6sec with 100mph (161kph) coming up in 15.4sec. True, the maxi-mum speed was just over 140mph (225kph) instead of the 150+ claimed by Lotus — the company's maximum speed claims were often optimistic — but for its handling, its ride, the vast improvements in finish, the crispness, smoothness and progressive response of its en-gine, it basked in accolade after accolade. The new chassis made the whole car feel much more rigid, though there were still some creaks, rattles and wind noise; now, it seemed, it was only these niggles which barred entry to the prestigious realms of Ferrari and Porsche.

An 'amphibious' Esprit had been James Bond's mount in the 1976 Bond epic *The Spy Who Loved Me*, and in 1981 it was the turn of the Turbo in *For Your Eyes Only*. The Lotus Esprit was on the map. Nothing much was to change until February 1987, when subtle engine changes brought yet

Above: Lotus has always been keen on 'limited edition' models, and in the past these have often reflected the F1 team's racing successes. The first Turbo Esprits were in the lurid livery of Essex Petroleum, but this rendering shows how a John Player turbo might have looked.

more power to the car.

That the car became the Turbo Esprit HC is the clue: a higher compression ratio, applied through-out the Lotus range. But there was more to it than just raising the compression ratio from 7.5:1 to 8.0:1. Maximum turbo boost pressure went up to 0.6bar (9.5psi), and the carburettors became larger-venturi Dellorto 45M DHLA. A smaller turbine housing improved low-speed throttle response, and a balance pipe improved cylinder-to-cylinder mixture distribution. Ports and inlet valve throats were enlarged and the exhaust manifold modified, and to keep the engine cool were higher-efficiency oil and water radiators and a higher-capacity water pump.

The result was a fractional power increase, from 210bhp at 650rpm to 215bhp at 6000rpm, but considerably more torque: 220lb ft at 4250rpm instead of 200 lb ft at the same speed. Subjected to *Motor*'s test routine, the HC man-aged 144mph (230kph), accelerated from a standstill to 60mph (97kph) in 5.4sec, and to 100mph (161kph) in 14.9sec. The Turbo Esprit HC, however, was to be a short-lived model, for the stage was set for the biggest change to the Esprit since its 1975 launch. Come 1987's Motor-fair at Earl's Court, all would be revealed.

SWEET SIXTEEN
Lotus's 900-series engines

Back in the mid-1960s, Lotus relied heavily on Ford for many components. Most important of these was the bottom half of the engine, a design which even then was no longer used in a current Ford in the form Lotus needed. The danger of Ford's cutting off supplies was one which worried Colin Chapman, who didn't like to be beholden to anyone. What Lotus needed was an engine of its own.

It would be a bigger engine, around 2 litres (122cu.in.) instead of the 1558cc (95cu.in.) Lotus was then using, so that Lotus could edge upmarket. It should embody up-to-the-minute technology, which meant an aluminium block and head with removable wet cylinder liners, twin belt-driven overhead camshafts, and four valves per cylinder. Bore/stroke dimensions would be oversquare, that is the bore diameter would be greater than the piston stroke.

As well as road use, the engine should be suitable for racing; and the design should allow the creation of a doubled-up V8 version with the same dual-purpose role. From the start, the four-cylinder unit would be designed to be mounted at a 45° longitudinal slant. The idea of a V6 engine had already been rejected on the grounds that it would be the wrong shape for the Lotus chassis; a 60° V6 would be too tall, a 120° one too wide.

Ron Burr, previously of racing engine manufacturer Coventry Climax, did the groundwork. Work began on the cylinder head first, and when to Lotus's great surprise the slant-four 2-litre Vauxhall engine, announced in October 1967, proved to have identical cylinder bore centres to Lotus's own proposal, Chapman quickly acquired some Vauxhall blocks. Lotus's cylinder head could easily be mounted on Vauxhall's cast-iron bottom end, which would greatly speed development.

THE FIRST ENGINES RUN
Lotus/Vauxhall hybrids

The resultant hybrid engines, completed in 1968, soon went racing in Lotus 62 sports-racing cars. In this form they were known as LV220, which simply meant Lotus-Vauxhall 220bhp – the racing engine's output. Its other identity was 904; numbers of 901 to 903 were never used in the 900 series. A road version followed, designated 905 and used in various Vauxhall cars and Bedford vans for development work, hotly pursued by the 906 engine whose sand-cast aluminium block severed the Vauxhall connection.

For quantity production, though, the block would need to be die-cast. Tony Rudd, fresh from BRM, was the man who made the engine a production reality, and it was ready in 1970 as the 907. There was not a Ford influence to be seen, and no Vauxhall parts within. That Vauxhall unwittingly helped in the engine's development is, with hindsight, ironic; Vauxhall's parent company, General Motors, bought Lotus in 1986.

So Lotus had an engine, but no car to put it in for it was too big for the existing range of Elans and Europas. At the same time, Kjell Qvale and Donald Healey, new owners of

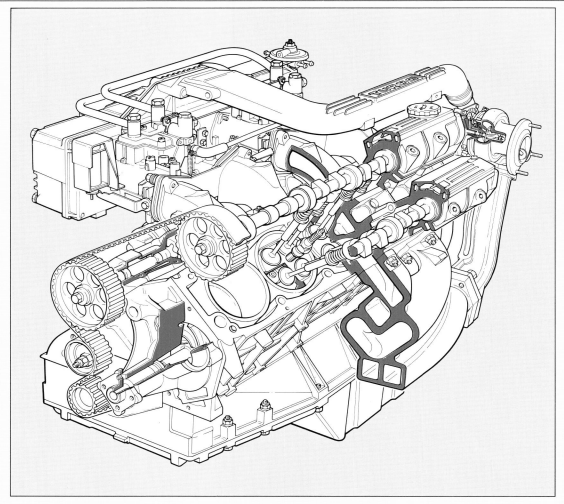

Above: Lotus's current 910 engine, with Dellorto 45M DHLA carburettors as fitted to current UK-spec Esprit *Turbos. The US version, with GM multipoint fuel injection, develops more power despite having a catalytic converter.*

Jensen Motors, were looking for an engine to power the forthcoming Jensen-Healey sports car. The deal was done, and production commenced in 1972 with the engine in 140bhp tune. Early examples had problems with oil accumulating around the valve gear and starving the oil pump because it couldn't drain back to the sump quickly enough, but this was soon solved. The Jensen/Lotus deal helped Lotus to struggle through the company's lean period, coming to an end in 1976 when Jensen ceased operations.

From 1974, of course, Lotus could put the engine in its own cars, but come 1979 a new derivative, the 911, appeared in the nose of a Chrysler (later Talbot) Sunbeam. The brainchild of Des O'Dell of Chrysler's competitions department, and developed by Lotus, the Chrysler Sunbeam Lotus was the first 900-series-powered car to use the longer-stroke crankshaft to give the current 2174cc (133cu.in.) capacity. However, it differed from the 912 engine later fitted to 2.2-litre normally aspirated Lotuses in a number of ways, in particular the design of its sump and main bearing panel.

In roadgoing trim, the engine delivered 155bhp; in rally trim, it typically gave 240bhp. Rallying was the reason for the car's existence, as a weapon against the all-conquering Escorts, and it did the job well: first in the 1980 RAC Rally, and the manufacturers' title in the 1981 World Rally Championship. Production ceased that year, after 2298 units.

THE VANISHING V8
Powerhouse with no home

Engine type 910 is the Turbo, as we have seen, so what of 908 and 909? These were two versions of Tony Rudd's 4-litre V8 engine, though neither got beyond the development stage. When the idea of a really quick Esprit was first suggested, there was much discussion as to whether to go to the expense of producing the V8, or instead to achieve an acceptable result for less outlay by turbocharging the existing engine. The latter approach won through, although even today you can sense a twinge of sadness at Lotus that the V8 Esprit never happened.

Mike Kimberley openly admits that the Turbo Esprit chassis was designed to take the V8, and hints that the project fell through because a major client, who would have bought engines from Lotus and thus make the whole idea financially viable, pulled out. For it to happen in the future there would need to be a collaborator. (An experimental Esprit V8 topped 170mph (273kph) before its driver, fearing for the tyres, backed off.)

It looked, at the 1984 British Motor Show, as though we *would* see a production Lotus powered by the V8, for on display was the Giugiaro-styled Etna concept car complete with 320bhp, 32-valve, 909 engine. There was talk of production by 1988 but, presumably because of the major client pulling out, the project was stillborn. Look at the latest Esprit, though, and you can't help but feel that some of the Etna's style has lived on.

So who was the major client? At the time, it was thought by industry watchers to be General Motors. If so, it's an interesting twist. The startlingly rapid new Chevrolet

Corvette ZR-1 is powered by a 5.7-litre (348cu.in.), 32-valve V8 dubbed LT5. And LT5, which delivers nearly 400bhp and 400lb ft of torque, was designed by Lotus. If you ask Tony Rudd what became of the Lotus V8, he points at a picture of the LT5 on his office wall . . .

TURBO DEVELOPMENT
The inside story
Graham Atkin was the man in charge of the turbo engine project, and a man staunchly in favour of lots of low-down torque. Mike Kimberley recalls how he and Atkin had to fight their case: 'Colin Chapman and Alan Curtis were all for top-end power, but we wanted the engine to feel like a big, multicylinder one. We won, and the result was so good that we were asked by seven other clients to do the same thing for them.'

Tony Rudd, now the Technical Director of Group Lotus and, at sixty-six, the grand old man of Hethel, takes up the tale. 'We were determined to go in the opposite direction from Porsche. We didn't want sudden death performance, we wanted it to be unobtrusive.

'We have a standard by which we measure turbo lag. You drive at 40 per cent of maximum speed, say 60mph in fourth or fifth, so the engine's in a steady state. Then you put your boot in, and measure the time to indicate 90 per cent of the rated boost. More than one second is unacceptable.

'Back in 1979,we couldn't afford fuel injection. So we decided to *blow* through the carburettors, to try to get the benefit of the latent heat of vapourisation of the fuel and get a degree of charge cooling. We had to put pressure seals on the throttle spindles, and make sure the fuel line pressure went up as the boost built up. Originally, high speeds used to knock holes in the pistons.

Below: Lotus's 4-litre V8, as seen in the 1984 Etna concept car, remains a stillborn project, but it forms the basis of the 5.7-litre, LT5 engine, *shown here, which powers Chevrolet's potent Corvette ZR-1. The camshafts are chain-driven, but otherwise the heritage is pure Lotus.*

Right: Group Lotus Technical Director Tony Rudd, ex-BRM, has been the man behind Lotus's engines since 1969. 'With *more charge cooling to allow higher boost pressures,' he says, 'the sky's the limit as far as ultimate power outputs are concerned.'*

'We actually had Bosch fuel injection back in 1982, ready for the US market. We did it to get through the 50,000-mile emission test requirement, but the Bosch airflow sensor couldn't cope with the amount of air that went through our engines. We had to modify it. When the Californians required on-board diagnostic ability, Bosch couldn't accommodate it so we went to an AC-Delco MPFI system. There's less airflow restriction, so more horsepower.'

AC-Delco, not surprisingly, is part of General Motors. There's another point about US-specification Turbo Esprits, too: before gaining fuel injection, they ran with the larger-venturi 45M DHLA carburettors later fitted to the Europeans' HC version. With a three-way catalytic converter and an auxiliary air pump, the engine still gave 205bhp and 194lb ft of torque. Performance was barely affected; Lotus is a world expert at building environment-friendly engines that pay practically no penalty in efficiency.

OF INJECTION AND INTERCOOLERS
Wastegates, too
The first Turbo Esprits had separate wastegates which were prone to foul the rear suspension and not work properly. For a time it was difficult to find suitable units, but Normalair Garrett, the Australian arm of Garrett AiResearch, eventually came up with the right one. Current cars have an integral wastegate which ovecomes the problem, plus watercooled turbocharger bearing which makes for much longer life – not surprising when you consider how hot the turbocharger gets.

In terms of Turbo development, there's a lot more to come yet. For example, the current US-specification car, with MPFI fuel injection and full electronic engine management, plus of course a catalytic converter,

actually produces *more* power than Britain's carburettor version: 218bhp at 6500rpm, backed up by 218lb ft of torque at 4000rpm. The German market is about to get that same engine, and logic suggests that all Esprits – indeed all Lotuses – will eventually have fuel injection.

Yet Tony Rudd can understand people's liking for the faithful carburettors that have served Lotus for so long. 'It's like going to see the shrink. People like to discuss their carburettors, to reset them every Saturday if they are so disposed. It keeps them happy.' What does Rudd think of the injected car? 'It lacks that eager jump-off. It's not measurable, but it's there. I put it down to that squirt of petrol you get from the accelerator pumps in the carbs.'

Rudd is also looking at variable-geometry turbochargers. These would give greater mid-range power at the expense of some at the top end; they would also get rid of the rather appealing, rattlesnake-like flutter from the wastegate on the overrun. Then there's electronic wastegate control . . . and intercoolers, which Lotus call chargecoolers.

So what of the chargecooler? You don't, of course, have to use air to cool the compressed petrol/air mix; you can use water as long as it's cooler than that which you are trying to cool down, and cool the water itself with a remote radiator. And this is exactly what is done in the Esprit Turbo SE, which was launched in both European and US markets in May 1989. The chargecooler is compact, and close enough to induction tract not to spoil the throttle response, while the chargecooler's own radiator is at the front of the car where the weight is beneficial and the airflow is strong. And it has MPFI fuel injection.

The effect is shattering. Power is up to 260bhp – 'The highest specific output [i.e. bhp/litre] of any production engine,' says a proud Mike Kimberley. What this means is 4.5sec to 60mph (97kph), 11.2sec to 100mph (161kph), and a top speed of 170mph (273kph). And Tony Rudd says there's more to come from Lotus's engine yet; as far as he's concerned, with bigger chargecoolers and more charge cooling, the sky's the limit.

THE ESPRIT TODAY

Today's Esprit is a very different animal from its 1975 forerunner; yet its modern, soft-edged form remains unmistakably Esprit

IN OCTOBER 1987, a newly confident Lotus unveiled the most immediate reason for this confidence: an Esprit so thoroughly re-engineered that it was almost a new car. Such was the importance of the US to Lotus, and so high were the hopes for the Esprit, that the shapely new Lotus was launched simultaneously both at the British Motorfair at London's Earl's Court, and in Florida.

The new car is as smooth and integrated as the old one had become sharp-edged and cluttered, as understated as its predecessor was brash. At last, here was an ultimate Lotus which hinted at the depths of ability beneath its exciting skin, instead of thwarting the onlooker with a superficial dazzle.

SURFACE ORIENTATION
Colin Spooner explains

Colin Spooner is Lotus's Director of Design. He was in charge of the later stages of the original Esprit's gestation; ten years on, he was the mastermind for the new car, project X180, too. He explains the thinking behind the Esprit's latest incarnation: 'The old car's shape was line-oriented. The new one is surface-oriented; its surfaces are integrated rather than being a collection of panels.

'With the previous car, the engineers had gradually added bits — which made it worse. There was no integration. Its proportions were stunning, but this disguised the clutter. If you looked at the details it was horrendous. You need to be able to photograph any little detail of the car and use it as an art form, like you can with a Porsche. With the old Esprit that had become impossible. We needed to give the car back its integrity.'

Remarkably, all the main dimensions of the new body are within 1in. (25mm) of the old one even though the car looks dramatically different. The change in styling philosophy deceives the eye with complete success. 'On the new car, the windscreen is curved, and instead of the bonnet valley there's a bulge. It looks more masculine. We also updated the bumpers: instead of plant-on bumpers, we used an integrated wraparound in their place.'

Below: The final full-size clay model of the restyled Esprit, from which the moulds were taken. Detail differences from production cars are the blacked-in triangles at the front edge of the quarter lights, the width of the front air intake, and the disc-style wheel design.

Yet, for all this, the new car remains unmistakably an Esprit. The low, shovel nose, the bonnet shutline cutting across the front directly behind the pop-up headlamp pods, the shape of the A-pillars (windscreen pillars) and of the side windows; these are some of the things that give an Esprit its characteristic identity, and they haven't changed.

HIGH-SPEED DEVELOPMENT
Ready in under two years

Instead of returning to Giugiaro, Lotus designed the new Esprit in-house. This way, the designers and engineers could work with each other in parallel, instead of one team having to wait until the other had finished. The benefits are obvious: greater control over each stage of the car's development, and – vitally important for Lotus at the time – a shorter gestation period.

Peter Stevens, Lotus's chief designer who once worked for the influential Ogle Design, is the man responsible for the new look. He has been treated as a Lotus employee ever since his 1984 Excel facelift, although he is, strictly speaking, a freelance designer. As well as continuing his Lotus work, Stevens remains a tutor at the Royal College of Art's automotive design school. 'It's a good stimulus for us,' says Spooner.

Stevens' sketches and a clay model were presented to the Lotus board in November 1985, at a time when the deal for General Motors to buy Lotus was in its closing stages, and with Lotus under GM ownership (though with operating independence guaranteed) in January 1986, X180 was given the green light. Development began under the auspices of Lotus Engineering, but with Lotus's consultancy business poised for dramatic expansion the company set up Lotus Design in June 1986.

Here, Stevens was joined by RCA graduates Julian Thomson, who carried out detail work on the Esprit's exterior, and Simon Cox who remodelled the interior. 'Originally we weren't going to change the interior at all, apart from giving it more head and foot room,' says Colin Spooner. 'Then we thought, "This is a new car, we can't put the old interior in". There was pressure to update it, so we redesigned it – minimally. There used to be a totally flying instrument panel [the boomerang pod]. It was a bit tacky, though, and it vibrated. The new one is more substantial, and the switchgear is more unified. The steering

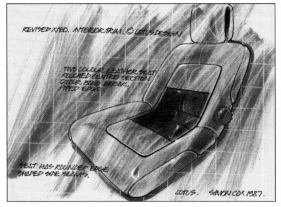
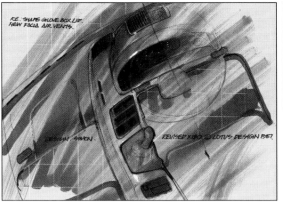
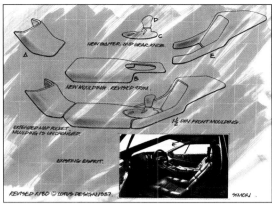

wheel is lower, too. Chapman's proportions were odd, which is why the old one was so high.'

Time was tight, but the design and engineering teams met Mike Kimberley's target of starting production by 1 August 1987. When the new Esprit Turbo (the words now reversed) and the normally aspirated Esprit (no longer bearing an S3 suffix) made their October debut, the reception was one of universal rapture. Even Giorgetto Giugiaro, to whose Etna concept car the new Esprit bore more than a passing resemblance, pronounced himself very pleased.

UK prices were set at £22,950 for the Esprit, £28,900 for the Turbo – increases over the final prices for the outgoing model of £2380 and £2920 respectively. For that increase, though, you were getting a vastly improved car. And it was still a good deal less expensive than the Ferrari 328 or Porsche 911 for which the Esprit was at last, a true rival.

So let us now look a little deeper beneath the Esprit's sleek new shape . . .

THE BODY
Smoother and stronger

Some of the results of the new body shape are not so visible. For example, with fewer sharp edges to act like hinges it is much more rigid despite being lighter: the new Esprit has 24 per cent greater torsional stiffness than the old car. This means that the suspension settings have had to be re-tuned slightly, as the springs are working against a more rigid structure. Not surprisingly, ride and handling are improved and the whole car feels a lot stiffer, more solid, than its somewhat squeak and rattle-prone predecessor. Stiffness to compare with that of a modern monocoque was the aim, and revised attachment points for the chassis have also played their part.

Above: Some early renderings by Simon Cox to show how the new interior might look. Virtually every aspect of the Esprit's interior *design was subjected to scrutiny as close as this. Notice how the revised car's internal factory codename, X180, appears on each sketch.*

The way the body is made, too, is dramatically different. The old Esprit body was designed to be made by Lotus's patented VARI process, but never was: 'We never had time,' says Mike Kimberley. The new one is, with consequent gains in speed and quantity of manufacture, and consistency of sizing and panel fit. There's still a ridge where the top and bottom halves of the shell are joined but, because the sections overlap vertically instead of abutting horizontally, the join is smoother and less protuberant.

Lotus prefers to describe the body as being of composite construction rather than merely glass-fibre, and with good reason. Around the roof opening and within the roof support pillars, much use is made of Kevlar aramid fibre which forms a structure of immense strength. In the US roof-crush test, designed to simulate a roll-over acci-

dent, the Esprit's roof deflected by just 1in. (25mm); the regulations allow 5in. (127mm).

There are other advantages of composite construction, too. The body won't rust, it will spring back into shape after a minor impact, and in a major impact it will collapse progressively with the damage remaining localised. However, if you deform a panel too far, by sitting on the bonnet for example, you will cause the resin gel coat to crack even though the panel itself will resume its shape. The problem is that the paint finish can hide the cracks – sometimes for as long as three months before they finally break through to the surface. By then it might be too late to claim on the insurance!

Below: The shape takes form. This is one of Peter Stevens' first renderings for the Esprit's new clothes, showing a softer, more rounded look but retaining essential elements of Giugiaro's original 1972 concept.

Bottom: Nearly there. The wraparound tail spoiler has been replaced by a simple lip, the midriff rib has been added and the sill has grown an air scoop. Compare this drawing with the clay model on the facing page.

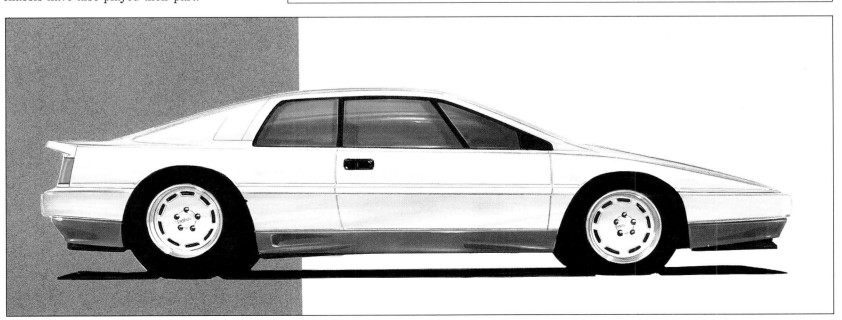

The glassfibre comes from three sources: Owens Corning, Pilkington and Vetrotex. International Paints, well-known in the yachting world, is one of the main suppliers of resin.

AERODYNAMICS
Stability over penetration
Purposeful looking vents and orifices abound over the Lotus's body. Both Turbo and normally aspirated versions now have scoops for cooling air at the rear end of the sills, and further engine compartment air enters through vents immediately aft of the rear side windows. Here, the old car had scoops which stood proud of the body, but now the body line is smooth and the windows' rear edges are recessed inwards. The depth of the recess forms the vent; that on the left is for further cooling, that on the right feeds the air filter and thence the engine's induction system.

The normally aspirated Esprit has a single, vertical rear window behind the cockpit, with the sloping rear upper body sides forming buttresses, Ferrari-fashion, either side of the flat bodywork above the engine. The rearmost section of the roof, the inner sides of the buttresses and the flat area between them, all open as one large tailgate to reveal a glassfibre engine cover and a luggage boot. On the Turbo, however, the upper two-thirds of the area between the buttresses is glassed in to form an extension of the roof, the remaining one-third forming a warm-air extraction slot. It's a much neater solution than the row of thick black louvres used in the old car, and it makes for a far clearer view aft when you look in the interior mirror.

That glass is the main reason why the Turbo has a better drag coefficient – 0.34 instead of 0.35 – than the lowlier Esprit, though differences in the design of the valance below the rear bumper play a part. Whereas the normal Esprit has two pairs of horizontal slots here, and a right-hand exhaust exit, the Turbo's fat, single pipe emerges on the left side above a faired-in under-bumper blade spoiler.

The previous Turbo, however, was officially credited with a 0.33 Cd, which caused great bafflement when the motoring press discovered that the new car's maximum speed was considerably higher. Unofficially, though, Peter Stevens has said that the old Turbo's Cd was actually over 0.40 by the end of its production run.

Now 0.34 is not a particularly impressive figure in itself – some production cars are now below 0.30 – but more important to Lotus was aerodynamic stability. By this is meant aerodynamic characteristics (such as lift) which remain constant, or which change in a progressive way, should the attitude of the car, or the direction of the wind, change. To get this right, Peter Stevens, his team and the Lotus shape spent 250 hours in two wind tunnels, one at Britain's Motor Industry Research Association near Nuneaton, the other at St Cyr in France.

BODY DETAILS
Small but significant
The body-colour front bumper, and its counterpart at the rear, are of RRIM (Reaction Resin Injection Moulded) plastic, which is flexible enough to absorb a 2.5mph (4kph) knock without damage. For US-specification cars, they are foam-filled which increases the front bumper's impact resistance enough to survive a 5mph (8kph) knock. Below the front bumper is a pair of rectangular fog lights (optional on the non-Turbo Esprit), above it are the retractable headlamp

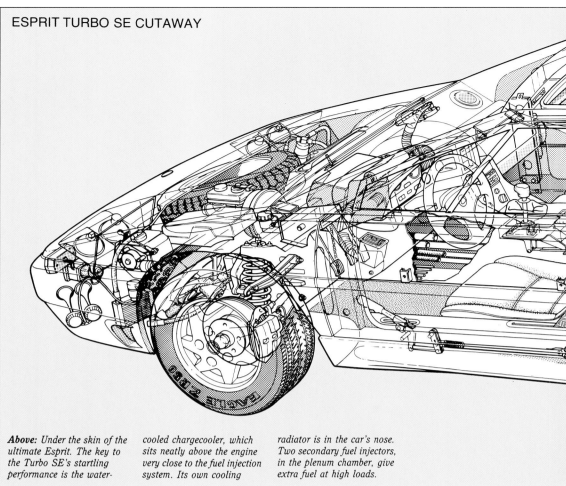

ESPRIT TURBO SE CUTAWAY

Above: Under the skin of the ultimate Esprit. The key to the Turbo SE's startling performance is the water-cooled chargecooler, which sits neatly above the engine very close to the fuel injection system. Its own cooling radiator is in the car's nose. Two secondary fuel injectors, in the plenum chamber, give extra fuel at high loads.

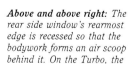

Above and above right: The rear side window's rearmost edge is recessed so that the bodywork forms an air scoop behind it. On the Turbo, the upper two-thirds of the area between the rear buttresses is glassed in, with the bottom one-third acting as a warm air extractor slot.

Below: Instead of the depressed centre panel in the bonnet of the old car, the current Esprit has a bulge. It makes the car look more muscular. This shot shows the wider under-bumper air intake, with foglights, compared with that of the clay model seen earlier.

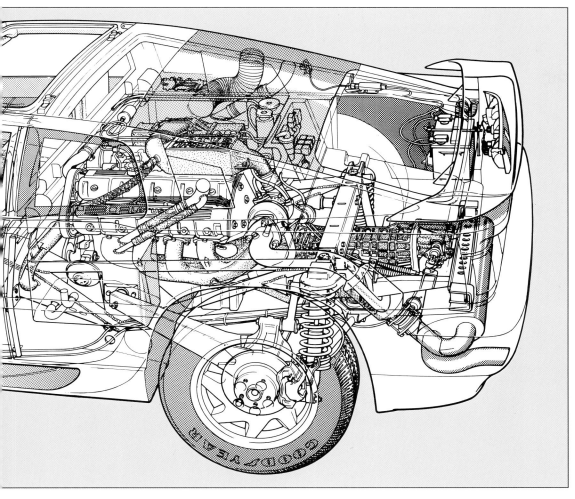

Above: Mirrors were intended to be faired into the triangular area in front of the quarter lights, but the resultant field of view was too narrow to comply with legislation, hence the production car's protuberant items. These mirrors are the improved, 1989-model versions.

pods. Switch on the headlamps, or flash them, and a powerful electric motor instantly raises the two pods which are linked by a cross shaft. Each pod contains two 6in. (152mm) halogen head-lamps, one for dipped beam and the other joining in for main beam.

Moving back along the car, you'll find the huge, single scissor-linkage windscreen wiper, now driven by a mechanical linkage instead of by cable, and able to sweep right up to the driver's-side edge of the windscreen. Like all the fixed glass, the windscreen is bonded into position as a structural member. Two single-jet washers keep it clean. Continuing rearwards, you'll meet a pair of large, protuberant but smoothly-shaped door mirrors. Lotus had hoped to fair them into the vacant triangular spaces forward of the front quarterlights, but positioned there they would give too small a field of view to satisfy legal requirements.

The glass in the door windows is the same as in the old shape car, but their frames are in steel instead of aluminium and now bear secondary seals to eradicate the oft-criticised wind noise. Extruded aluminium beams within the doors give protection against side impacts, and form attachment points for the hinges. There is a good reason for retaining the 'mousetrap' door handles outside and inside, dated though they might look; they are among the items closely scrutinised by the Americans when certifying a car's compliance with their complex safety legislation, and changing the door handles would have involved great expense in re-certification bills.

With Kevlar reinforcement making the perimeter of the roof so strong, it was easy for Lotus to

engineer a roof panel which can be either tilted for extra ventilation or removed altogether. As standard this is made of Nomex – an epoxy-impregnated paper honeycomb, supplied by CIBA-Geigy – with a glassfibre and resin skin on each side, but a tinted glass panel is optional. If you want an open Esprit, you can store the roof panel in the rear luggage compartment protected by its tailored bag. A removable wind deflector, normally kept in the bag, fits into place behind the windscreen header rail to prevent draughts. It's the next best thing to a convertible.

The twin fuel fillers, one on each side of the car behind the rear side windows and opening into separate but linked tanks, are now opened from inside the car by a solenoid switch. Moving further back, we find a gentle tail spoiler perfect-ly integrated into the shape of the car's rump. It's actually a separate component, and sits above big, bold horizontal tail light clusters which, unlike the Rover SD1 units of the old car, do not shout their origins. Subtly styled, in fact they are Toyota items.

CHASSIS, SUSPENSION, STEERING
Much as before

Fundamentally unchanged in the new car, the backbone chassis is not particularly rigid in its own right. Once it is bolted to the body, though, the combined stiffness is practically double that of the chassis alone. Greater structural rigidity than in the old Esprit means that Lotus has been able to use softer suspension, and thus gain a smoother ride, without sacrificing roadholding ability. That said, the springs themselves are actually very similar in stiffness to those of the old car, the softer suspension being a result of combining those springs with the new car's greater overall weight. In the case of the Turbo, this is up from 2646lb (1200kg) to 2793lb (1268kg), distributed 43 per cent on the front wheels and 57 per cent on the rear wheels.

Front suspension is a classic double unequal-length wishbone system. The upper, shorter wishbone is made from a pair of channel-section steel pressings; the lower one consists of a box-section steel transverse link to which is welded,

Right: Aerodynamic refinements on the Esprit Turbo include a moulded lip spoiler situated above the tail light panel, and a further spoiler below the rear bumper which is shaped to form an air outlet. The transverse exhaust silencer is visible behind it.

at the hub carrier end, a forward-angled tubular steel arm to make a strong, triangulated unit. The reason for the difference in the wishbones' length is to ensure correct wheel camber as the car leans during cornering. The arms of the upper wishbone pass either side of a coil spring/telescopic twin-tube damper unit, which fits between the lower wishbone and the chassis frame.

Projecting forward from the lower wishbone's outer end is the anti-roll bar, joined to the wishbone by a large rubber bush and angled in towards the extreme front of the chassis. From there the bar runs across the front of the chassis frame, clamped to it by two rubber bushes, and turns back towards the other lower wishbone.

Prior to 1985, there was no lower wishbone as such although the geometry was similar. Instead, there was merely a transverse link, which was located fore and aft by the anti-roll bar.

At the rear, the geometry is similar though it is achieved in a different way. The alloy hub carrier is located at its upper end by a transverse link made out of steel tube, and a similar, but longer and slightly rearward-pointing, tube anchors the carrier's lower end. This time, of course, the hub carrier does not swivel as there is no steering movement to accommodate.

A co-axial coil spring/damper unit fits between the rear edge of the hub carrier and the stout cross member that runs across the upper rear of the chassis, while pivoted on the front edge of the hub carrier is a substantial box-section arm. This semi-trailing radius arm points forwards and inwards to pivot near the front of the tubular engine cradle. Most of the steel suspension components, front and rear, are cadmium-plated, and there is half a degree of negative camber at each wheel.

Steering is by conventional rack and pinion, with the track rods emerging from each end of the rack and operating on the forward side of the swivelling hub carriers. No power assistance is considered necessary, as most of the Esprit's weight is taken by the rear wheels. The rack gives a steering ratio of 15.4:1, equivalent to exactly three turns from one extreme of lock to the other for a turning circle of 36ft (11m).

By positioning the front hub carrier's top swivel slightly further back than the bottom swivel, the axis around which the front wheel steers slopes back by 2° 30'; this castor angle helps the steering to self-centre and to give feedback to the driver. The axis also inclines inwards as you follow it upwards, at 9° 20'.

BRAKES
All change
The Esprit now has ventilated front disc brakes. They are Toyota items of 10in. (258mm) diameter and 0.8in. (20mm) thickness, with ventilation by radial fins sandwiched by the outer and inner braking surfaces. Their calipers are mounted behind the wheel centres.

There's change at the rear, too. A Renault transaxle has replaced the Citroën one (except in 1988 model year US-specification cars),

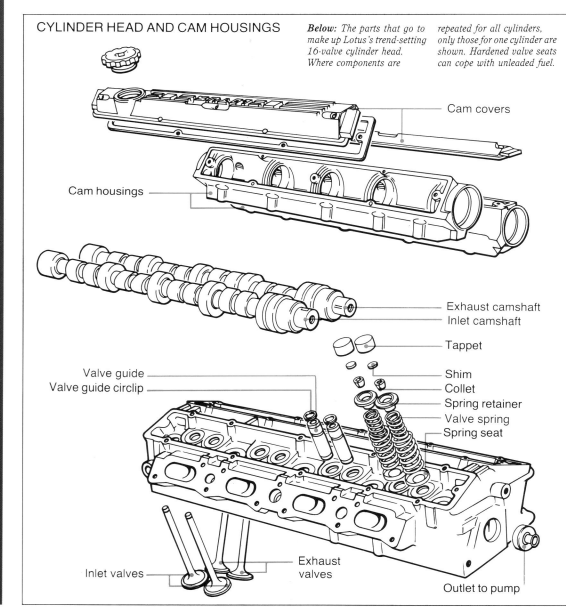

CYLINDER HEAD AND CAM HOUSINGS

Below: The parts that go to make up Lotus's trend-setting 16-valve cylinder head. Where components are repeated for all cylinders, only those for one cylinder are shown. Hardened valve seats can cope with unleaded fuel.

- Cam covers
- Cam housings
- Exhaust camshaft
- Inlet camshaft
- Tappet
- Valve guide
- Valve guide circlip
- Shim
- Collet
- Spring retainer
- Valve spring
- Spring seat
- Inlet valves
- Exhaust valves
- Outlet to pump

Above: This is a prototype US-specification Turbo Esprit, with the earlier four-spoke wheels and no air duct on the sill. The body shell was modified to give extra head and leg room for the American market. Sold by Lotus Performance Cars from 1982, it marked Lotus's US rebirth.

Above: The Current US-market Esprit Turbo, finished as standard with silver-grey lower body panels, with its amber side lamps and illuminated side markers. More significantly it also has a fuel-injected engine, which gives more power despite its emissions equipment.

setting-up of a limited partnership with fifty partners each contributing $100,000, to import and distribute the Esprit and be named Lotus Performance Cars, Lotus quickly set about adapting the Turbo Esprit to Federal specification.

Indeed, the end result was not far from being a new car, because the body moulds were altered to give more head and leg room in the cabin. The normally aspirated S3 gained similar modifications, enough to earn the Federal version the new designation of S4. In December 1982, the month Colin Chapman died, Lotus Performance Cars opened its doors in New Jersey; the sad irony was that no fewer than 184 Federal Esprits were made the following year, a fact which was to be one of the key ingredients of Lotus's recovery.

THE GRAND PLAN
Lotus buys out LPC

'You've got to run your own operation if it's to be a success.' Those are Mike Kimberley's words, and they explain why, in December 1986, Lotus bought out its US importer. The grand plan, which is beginning to work out with the impressive sales success of the new-shape Esprit, hinges on the introduction of the higher-volume M100, or Elan, to the US – and it's a plan which Lotus cannot afford to let fail. There's been considerable expansion since the December 1986 formation of Lotus Cars USA Inc., with the number of dealers up from fifty-two to seventy-four and a headquarters move to Lawrenceville, near Atlanta, Georgia. By the Elan's launch, there will be ninety.

Sales, currently of turbocharged Esprits only, are booming, and US customers can even have a leasing deal arranged through the Chase Manhattan bank. It's a long way from the dark days of 1982: this time, Lotus seems to have got it right.

ESPRIT PRODUCTION

	UK	Federal	Euro Federal	RoW
1976	134	4	–	–
1977	71	474	–	35
1978	254	251	–	48
1979	269	128	–	77
1980	99	13	–	25
1981	233	17	–	51
1982	262	3	–	100
1983	201	184	–	42
1984	301	174	–	47
1985	292	108	–	51
1986	117	215	36	73
1987	205	166	30	59
1988*	401	393	76	96
Total	2839	2130	142	704

* To November
Grand total of Esprit production is 5815.

Figures are totals which take in all Esprit variants, both Turbo and normally aspirated.

Federal = US specification, though a few examples have been sold in Japan.

Euro Federal = European cars for countries where catalytic converters are the norm, e.g. Switzerland and West Germany.

RoW = Rest of World

Below: This was to be a cheap, basic, US-only version of the Esprit, powered by the 2.3 litre, 180bhp GM Quad-4 engine. Mike Kimberley disliked the idea of a non-Lotus-powered Lotus, so the top half of the body was changed to give a new identity.

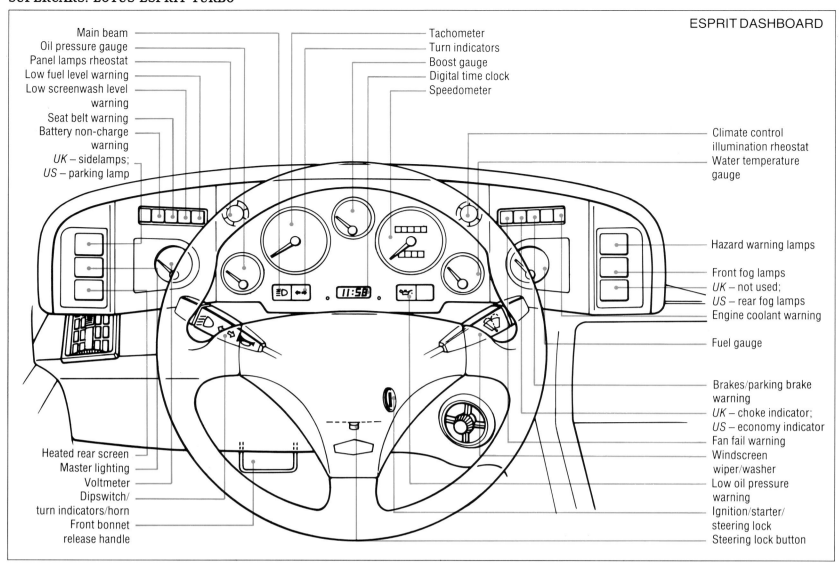

ESPRIT DASHBOARD

Main beam
Oil pressure gauge
Panel lamps rheostat
Low fuel level warning
Low screenwash level warning
Seat belt warning
Battery non-charge warning
UK – sidelamps;
US – parking lamp

Tachometer
Turn indicators
Boost gauge
Digital time clock
Speedometer

Climate control illumination rheostat
Water temperature gauge

Hazard warning lamps
Front fog lamps
UK – not used;
US – rear fog lamps
Engine coolant warning

Fuel gauge

Brakes/parking brake warning
UK – choke indicator;
US – economy indicator
Fan fail warning
Windscreen wiper/washer
Low oil pressure warning
Ignition/starter/ steering lock
Steering lock button

Heated rear screen
Master lighting
Voltmeter
Dipswitch/ turn indicators/horn
Front bonnet release handle

which has led to the adoption of outboard, but still solid, discs of 10.8in. (275mm) diameter and 0.5in. (12mm) thickness mounted within the rear wheels. These brakes are of Bendix manufacture, as is the master cylinder which actuates a dual, front/rear-split, hydraulic circuit via a direct-acting vacuum servo. The first year's production of US market cars retained their inboard rear brakes, positioned either side of the Citroën transaxle. The handbrake operates the rear calipers via cables.

WHEELS AND TYRES
Surprisingly high aspect ratio
For supercars, tyre aspect ratios (the ratio of sidewall height to tread width) are often 50 per cent or even lower. But the Esprit bucks the trend with Goodyear Eagle NCT tyres of 195/60 VR 15 dimensions at the front, and 235/60 VR 15 at the rear. This is done in the interests of ride quality and the knowledge that the chassis can exploit the tyres' characteristics – developed jointly by Goodyear and Lotus at Goodyear's technical centre in Luxembourg – to the full.

These tyres are mounted on seven-spoke alloy wheels, 7JK×5in. at the front and 8JK×15in. at the rear, made to Lotus's design by OZ Italia. Owing to the different transaxle and rear brake specifications, 1988 model year US-specification cars had greater rear wheel offset (that is, the wheel centres were recessed further into the wheel) to achieve the same rear track width.

Normal pressures are 21psi front and 25psi rear, but continuous running over 120mph (193kph) calls for 30psi all round. The 175/ 70 SR 14 Goodyear Grand Prix S-shod spare wheel,

stored in the front compartment, is for emergency use only and should not be used at speeds above 50mph (80kph).

ENGINE
Well-proven power
The Esprit's 2174cc (132.7 cu.in.), four-cylinder, twin-overhead-camshaft, 16-valve engine now develops 215bhp at 6000rpm, and 220lb ft of torque at 4250rpm, when turbocharged and running on Dellorto 45M DHLA carburettors. With an 8.0:1 compression ratio, that's the current specification for most of Europe. However, in low-emission US 'Federal' specification, as will gradually be adopted in Europe as well, the Turbo engine is now actually more potent with 228bhp at 6500rpm, and 218lb ft of torque at 4000rpm. In this guise, new for 1989, it runs on AC-Delco multipoint fuel injection (MPFI) with Lotus's own electronic engine management programme (replacing the previous Bosch K-Jetronic system), plus the obligatory three-way (hydrocar-

bons, nitrogen oxides and carbon monoxide) catalytic converter.

Without a turbocharger, and again running on carburettors but this time a 10.9:1 compression ratio, the 912S engine of the normally aspirated Esprit delivers 172bhp at 6000rpm, and 163lb ft of torque at 5000rpm. Carburettor-fed cars, turbocharged or not, will run on either 97-octane leaded or Eurosuper 95-octane unleaded fuel; cars with catalytic converters must use unleaded fuel only.

Aluminium die-castings are used for most of the non-moving parts of the engine, including the sump. The removable, wet (because they are surrounded by coolant) cylinder liners, also of aluminium, are made by the German piston firm Mahle; they are coated on the inside with hard-

Below: Not much room for luggage under the bonnet – the space is all but filled by the fluid reservoirs, fuses, relays, headlamp motors, *brake servo, toolkit and the 175/70 SR 14 Goodyear Grand Prix S space tyre mounted on a steel wheel rim. A gas strut holds the lid open.*

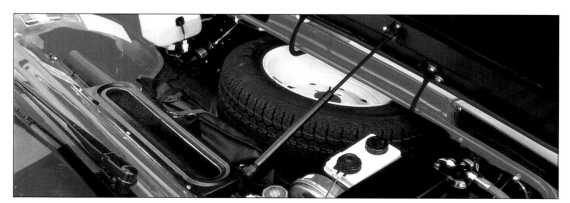

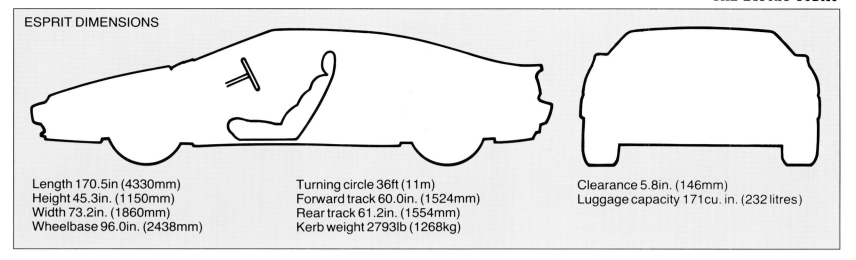

ESPRIT DIMENSIONS

Length 170.5in (4330mm)
Height 45.3in. (1150mm)
Width 73.2in. (1860mm)
Wheelbase 96.0in. (2438mm)

Turning circle 36ft (11m)
Forward track 60.0in. (1524mm)
Rear track 61.2in. (1554mm)
Kerb weight 2793lb (1268kg)

Clearance 5.8in. (146mm)
Luggage capacity 171cu. in. (232 litres)

wearing Nikasil (a nickel and silicon carbide mix). Each liner's bore is 3.75in. (95.3mm) across; each throw of the forged steel, five-bearing crankshaft gives a piston stroke of 3in. (76.2mm). The caps for these five main bearings, instead of being separate, are joined in one rigid main bearing panel for extra strength.

Each of the cylinder head's four combustion chambers is of pent-roof shape, each face of the 'roof' housing two inlet valves (on the engine's right side) or two exhaust valves (on the left side) which are serviced by ports on the relevant side. In the centre of the chamber are the electrodes of an NGK spark plug, fired a minimum of 10° of crankshaft rotation before the piston reaches top dead centre on the compression stroke.

In the Turbo, the exhaust valves are sodium-filled and run in Hidural 5 guides for better heat dissipation. Valve clearances are adjusted by varying the thickness of hardened steel shims between the valve stem and the inverted-bucket cam followers, or tappets – a method used for years on racing engines, and still best for a high-

efficiency unit when maintenance costs are not too important.

These tappets are actuated, and the valves opened, by belt-driven camshafts: one for the inlet valves, one for the exhausts. Each sits in its own five-bearing housing, topped by a finned red cam cover. An auxiliary shaft, itself driven by the same internally-toothed belt, drives the oil pump and ignition distributor. Ignition is electronic, with no contact-breaker, forming part of the computerised ignition/fuel injection system in MPFI-equipped cars.

The Turbo's exhaust manifold is now of stainless steel. It incorporates the revised Garrett AiResearch T3 turbocharger, with integral wastegate and water-cooled centre bearing to stop the oil carbonising when the hot engine is switched off and oil flow has stopped. It leads into a substantial silencer, which is positioned across the rear of the car behind the under-bumper valance.

Fuel for the Turbo's engine is fed from the right-hand fuel tank to a high-pressure turbine-

type fuel pump capable of delivering 22 gallons (100 litres) per hour. It is then pumped, via a canister fuel filter, to the fuel pressure regulating valve mounted on the rear of the plenum chamber positioned over the carburettor intake mouths. A spring and diaphragm system in the regulating valve maintains fuel pressure at 0.27bar (4psi) above turbo boost pressure to ensure a constant supply.

Excess fuel is returned to the top of the right-hand tank; this continuous circulation of fuel helps prevent vapour locks in hot conditions. A balance pipe linking the bases of the two fuel tanks ensures the level stays the same in both, and an inertia switch cuts the fuel pump's electrical supply in an impact.

TRANSMISSION
Still French

To safeguard future supplies for the envisaged increase in Esprit production rates, Lotus decided to look for a new source of supply for transaxles. This was found in the shape of the

RENAULT UN1-16 TRANSMISSION

Below: Instead of the old Citroën SM unit, the Esprit now uses a Renault UN1-16 transmission as also found in its French rival, the Renault Alpine or GTA. It is a conventional five-speed, two-shaft, all-indirect unit with three-rail selectors and an intricately cast, all-aluminium casing with many strengthening webs.

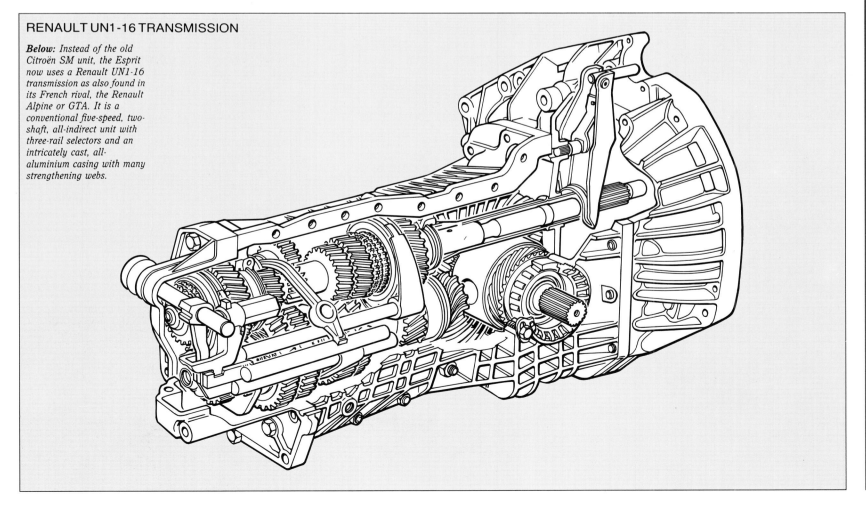

Renault UN1-16 unit, as used in the front of the Renault 25 and the rear of the GTA/Alpine but with the combination of ratios slightly altered to Lotus's requirements. It's a fairly conventional two-shaft unit; the clutch drives the top shaft, which passes above the differential, with drive then travelling through one of the five pairs of gears, or the reverse gear train, to exit forwards, via the bottom shaft, into the differential.

All five forward gears have synchromesh engagement. The gear lever is linked to the transaxle via two push-pull cables, attached to selector shafts within the transaxle. Fore-and-aft lever movements make each cable move in the same direction, transverse movements in opposing directions. Thus, each lever position gives a unique position of the cables relative to each other and to the transaxle casing, which enables the selector shafts to engage the gears.

To spread the costs of Federal re-certification, the first year's production of US-specification Esprits retained the earlier, and 20lb (9kg) heavier, five-speed Citroën transmission. This has a lower torque capacity, insufficient to cope with the power of the 1989 model year US Esprits, so all cars now have the Renault transaxle. It drives through a 9.25in. (235mm) single-plate diaphragm-spring clutch, hydraulically operated.

INTERIOR
Many refinements

The new bodyshell gives a roomier cockpit. While the gains – 0.8in. (20mm) in headroom, 1in. (25mm) in the width of each footwell, and 0.6in. (15mm) in legroom – might seem small in themselves, the effect on perceived spaciousness is considerable. The seats, too, are wider (by 1in./25mm). As standard they are trimmed in tweed, with transverse leather inserts – of contrasting hue in the Turbo – which are repeated on the centre tunnel and in a diagonal leather stripe within the tweed door panel inserts.

Leather also covers most of the rest of the interior, carpets apart, coloured to match the main body of the seat. Except, that is, for the black of the instrument binnacle, the upper half of the sloping fascia panel and the steering wheel

Below: An early rendering for the new and devastatingly quick Turbo SE. This intercooled – or, more correctly, chargecooled – car is the ultimate development of the Esprit to date. In practice the styling changes are slightly less dramatic than shown here.

Above: Interior of one of the forty limited edition Turbos produced from October 1988 to mark Lotus's 40th anniversary. Two-tone blue leather is complemented by blue suede, with the instruments set in a burr elm panel. The Sony hi-fi system includes a compact disc player.

– three-spoke in the Turbo, two-spoke in the normally aspirated Esprit. The leather fits snugly, without the overblown, over-ruched, slightly home-made look of the previous car.

Cabin storage space is minimal, consisting merely of a large fascia glove-box. Its sloping lid is opened by pressing down on the lower edge to release the catch. The stereo system, sitting in the top of the centre console, will be a Clarion one if it was fitted with the factory's blessing; beneath it are the controls for the heater system (now with a quieter and more powerful fan) or, if fitted, Lotus's own air-conditioning system. Cabin air now exits via vents in the doors, instead of through separate, and less efficient, rear extractors behind the cabin's occupants.

Cool air is available from four fascia vents regardless of the heater's temperature setting: the outer, grid-pattern pair admits fresh air only, while the inner, eyeball-pattern pair admits fresh or recirculated air according to the heater distribution settings. Recirculated air is a great benefit in traffic, since it means you can avoid

sucking in exhaust fumes from the car in front.

The new VDO instruments, with electronic operation for the turbo boost and oil pressure gauges, have white-on-black calibrations which are bathed at night in a soft green light. Interspersed among them is a full complement of warning lights, with their own automatic self-check facility. This is triggered when the ignition is first switched on, and cancelled once the engine is running. The push/push switches on the extreme left and right of the binnacle, which control all lights plus the heated rear window, are illuminated when the appropriate function is in use. For night driving, this illumination intensifies the existing background lighting of the switch symbols.

Lightweight Ristex wiring links all the electrical components, protected by thirty-six fuses instead of the previous model's eight.

ESPRITS WITH A DIFFERENCE
Colour schemes, limited editions

In Europe, the standard finish is one colour all over, though at extra cost you can have the sills and under-bumper valances finished in metallic silver grey. In the United States, however, this contrasting lower-body colour is standard and you have to pay extra to have a one-colour Esprit!

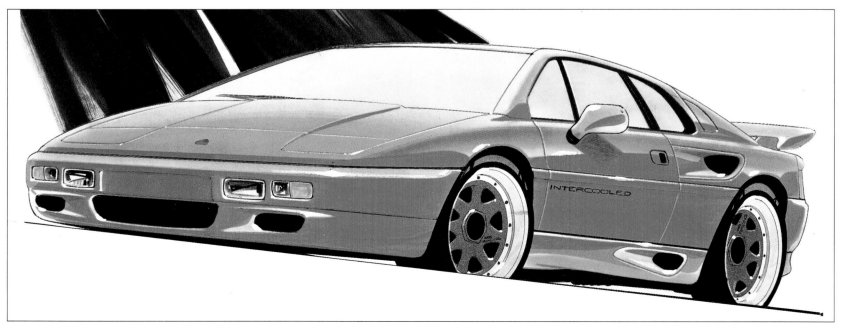

Such are the forces of marketing.

The first new-shape Esprit Turbos delivered to US customers were all-over pearlescent white Limited Edition models, with matching white wheels and a bold rear wing. Just eighty-eight were released to mark the model year of the new car's introduction. Then, at the 1988 British Motor Show, Lotus announced a limited run of forty special Esprit Turbos to mark Lotus's 40th anniversary. These cars, destined mainly for the UK market, were again in pearlescent white. That bold rear wing was complemented, this time, by a deep front spoiler.

Inside, two-tone blue Connolly leather and grey suede covered the seats, console, door trims and roof lining, while the instruments were set in a polished burr elm veneer panel. A Sony CDX A20 CD player, with a 10-disc autochange, was linked to an XR7200 stereo radio/cassette player, an XM601 amplifier, an XE8 seven-band graphic equaliser and six speakers, the whole rejoicing under the highly appropriate title of Disc Jockey. Air conditioning and telephone wiring were standard, and each car bore an individually-numbered, hallmarked silver commemorative plaque on the fascia.

ESPRIT TURBO SE
The ultimate Esprit – so far

As this was being written, the chargecooled Esprit Turbo SE was shaping up for its May 1989 launch. As well as its massively powerful engine, it features changes in front suspension geometry for lighter steering with improved feel, better handling balance and more progressive responses. The 15 per cent anti-dive geometry of the standard car has been changed to 20 per cent pro-dive, castor angle is halved but the steering trail angle is increased to maintain some self-centring. Front dampers and springs are recalibrated.

Despite Goodyear Eagle VR unidirectional tyres with an ultra-low-profile 50 per cent aspect ratio, better able than the 60-profile NCTs to cope with the extra power and speed, the ride is said to be even smoother. Front tyres are 215/50 ZR 15, with 245/50 ZR 16 on the rear, while the brakes are uprated with Ferodo 3432 disc pad material. This has the same coefficient of friction, but much higher resistance to fade. Aerodynamic improvements include a deep front spoiler with air exit ducts, and a wraparound spoiler beneath the rear bumper. Between them they ensure not only a downforce at 100mph (161kph), but one which is balanced front to rear.

Roger Becker speaks enthusiastically of the new car. 'We have calmed the car's initial response a bit, and given it greater linearity of response. The normal Esprit goes into roll oversteer, so when you turn into a bend there's a two stage response: understeer is followed, under hard cornering, by roll oversteer. The chargecooled car has gentle roll understeer, so it corners with one flowing response.

'Because there's more grip, we can use the mid-engined configuration's inherent edge of instability to advantage. We can get a better balance, so you can alter the car's cornering attitude from a neutral stance rather than from the understeering attitude we felt we had to build into the standard car. So you can change the car's attitude mid-corner more easily in the intercooled car, whether by steering or throttle.

'This is a car developed by drivers, for drivers to appreciate. It's got the fastest chassis response characteristics ever recorded in the motor industry.'

Above and below: As this book went to press we were able to have one of the first drives in the quickest Esprit of all. Final performance figures for the Turbo SE, fitted with what is more accurately termed a chargecooler than an intercooler, are 0–60mph in 4.7sec, 0–100mph in 11.5sec, and a maximum speed of 163mph. And that is on unleaded fuel, with a catalytic converter, and producing just half the exhaust emissions legally allowed in the US.

The engine, nominally capable of 264bhp at 6500rpm and 261lb ft of torque at 3900rpm, can deliver up to 280bhp for bursts of 30 seconds. Sophisticated electronics monitor every engine parameter including the distributorless direct ignition system, and maximum boost pressure is raised slightly to 0.85bar (12.4psi). When the engine is cold, this is automatically reduced to 0.65bar (9.4psi).

The chargecooler's water circuit is separate from that of the radiator, because the operating temperatures and flow requirements differ. Water is circulated by a rubber-vaned pump located where the distributor used to be found, to a heat exchanger in the car's nose ahead of the air-conditioning condenser and the engine radiator. Twin oil coolers flank this sandwich, the whole being cooled by air admitted through the redesigned under-bumper air intakes.

These, with their wire mesh grilles, bring the welcome return of an almost Elan-like 'face': the frontal aspect is very purposeful. So, too, are the enlarged air scoops in the sills, the rear wing and the fat, low-profile Eagle ZR tyres specially developed for the SE. There's leather trim and a burr elm instrument panel inside.

Driving the SE is a revelation. The engine is even smoother than before, and quieter too, with performance similar in character except there's yet more of it. We lapped Millbrook at 158.7mph, a speed at which we were probably losing around 5mph in tyre scrub. It's an engine completely without temperament, free of the carburettor-fed car's hot-start histrionics, and with untainted progression of turbo boost as you are launched towards the horizon.

As for the handling, all the standard car's good points are retained, or improved upon, all the less good ones are banished. The steering, for example, has lost its heaviness and overly-strong self centring to become light, crisp and transparently informative; the handling balance has lost the artificial understeer which gave way to oversteer, to be replaced by one long, flowing, sweep through the most challenging of bends.

The Esprit Turbo was brilliant to begin with. The SE borders on the incredible. Of its importance, Mike Kimberley had this to say: 'The new Lotus Esprit Turbo SE is a significant step for the marque in setting new world standards in ride, handling, balance, engine output and total vehicle performance.'

KIMBERLEY AT THE HELM
Lotus, post-Chapman

Colin Chapman's death in 1982 was a terrible blow. Lotus was in deep trouble, and sorely needed its founder's fighting spirit. But that spirit must have rubbed off on Lotus's corporate consciousness, because once again the company bounced back.

Fred Bushell was the accountant who had joined Colin Chapman's new Lotus company, founded with a £25 loan (early 1989 rates, about $50) from Chapman's wife-to-be, back in 1953. His rôle, right from the start, had been to temper Chapman's enthusiasm with an eye for financial reality, and as the founder's greatest ally he was the obvious heir to the chairmanship.

This was at a time when Lotus's future was looking rosier than it had for some while. Sales were picking up, the company had just re-entered the US market, and the public showing of the revolutionary active suspension (developed by Team Lotus's Peter Wright) maintained Lotus's faith in its innovative engineering. But the problem of cash flow remained, following American Express's withdrawal; there was little interest in the financial community in taking on the Lotus debts, despite the company's burgeoning image of high technology. By the end of March, the problem looked terminal.

NEW BACKERS
And upheavals within

Both Mike Kimberley and Alan Curtis (the latter an ex-Aston Martin man who had also tried to put the MGB back into production) had been directors of Lotus Cars, but not of the Group Lotus parent company which also controlled the Lotus Engineering consultancy. This quickly changed, and they joined Fred Bushell and Peter Kirwan-Taylor on the main board. Meanwhile Toyota gave financial help, and Alan Curtis began negotiations with David Wickins, the founder of British Car Auctions.

Wickins saw the vast potential of the engineering division, and by June 1983 a re-financing package saw British Car Auctions holding a 25 per cent stake in Lotus, Toyota with 23 per cent, and merchant bankers Schroeder-Wagg with 10 per cent. At last, reinvestment could commence with Lotus Engineering first in line. The profits from the expanded engineering department could then finance expansion, and new model development, on the car side.

In 1984, with the De Lorean scandal still simmering, Fred Bushell left to devote himself full-time to his chairmanship of Team Lotus – which remains in Hazel Chapman's ownership. Peter Kirwan-Taylor, too, sensed that the thread tying him to the rapidly changing Lotus was fraying, and from the scene to concentrate on his City interests. JCB, the excavator company, gained a 12 per cent holding, and a business associate of David Wickins acquired a 14 per cent block of shares. Mike Kimberley, meanwhile, became chief executive and managing director, a position he holds to this day.

Wickins, by then effectively the executive chairman, was in a strong position to exercise his will. One result of this was the

change in design of the Lotus badge; the new, squashed-teardrop one had the letters overlapping and – to the great consternation of all those who held Chapman's memory dear – no ACBC monogram. It was a controversial act, and the board was far from unanimous in its approval. Within a short time, the monogram was restored to its rightful position before too much goodwill was squandered. Team Lotus, of course, retained the original round badge.

ENTER GENERAL MOTORS
An end to under-investment

By mid-1985, with the proportions of Lotus shares held by the various shareholders altered slightly, Lotus looked to be on a sounder footing than ever before in its history. But, in order to fund the new car (which had developed from M90 to become X100), and to modernise the existing range (notably the Esprit), it became clear to the board that Lotus was going to have to seek the backing of a major car compay – to a greater degree than Toyota was prepared to consider.

Alan Curtis, who is now the non-executive chairman, discovered that Lotus had many potential suitors; but, in the end, a deal was struck with Bob Eaton, vice-president of General Motors, whereby GM would acquire a majority (58 per cent) shareholding from the Schroeder-Wagg/BCA/JCB block. By 22 January 1986, the deal was done. In May, GM bought Toyota's share (though Toyota would continue to supply components for existing model ranges), by October it had a

Above: Michael Kimberley, chief executive and managing director of Group Lotus. While Lotus has an enthusiast like him at the helm, backed up by General Motors' financial muscle, its future is rosy.

91 per cent stake, and from there it was a short path to the total ownership of today.

The Group Lotus board is now seven-strong, with two non-executive GM mem-

bers (Eaton and John Smith) and five Britons. In addition, each of the four constituent companies – Lotus Cars, Lotus Engineering, Lotus Design and Lotus Cars USA Inc – has its own directors; the managing director of Lotus Engineering, for example, is Peter Wright, who is the father of the Active Suspension concept.

Outside Lotus and GM, fears were widespread that Lotus would lose its independence and its identity after the GM takeover. After all, how could a giant like GM fail to crush a fragile flower like Lotus? The pundits have been proved absolutely wrong. Lotus has even, as of October 1988, reverted to Colin Chapman's original, round, green and yellow Lotus badge as a fitting way to mark the Lotus name's fortieth anniversary.

LOTUS BLOSSOMS
The Kimberley philosophy

Mike Kimberley, the tall, open, direct-speaking engineer and car enthusiast whose job it is to steer Lotus into the future, plays down the GM connection. 'We're far more independent than ever before. General Motors bought shares, but no more equity, and Group Lotus borrows from British banks.

'We've got a unique culture here, innovative and creative. Creativity is a fragile and delicate thing.' The inference is clear: if GM values Lotus's creativity, it had better leave Lotus alone and be content with the profits.

Michael John Kimberley, who looks younger than his fifty years, joined Lotus in 1969 from Jaguar, where he had been a design and development engineer. One of his projects there was the beautiful, never-to-be-raced XJ13 mid-engined Le Mans contender. At Lotus, his first project was the Europa Twin-Cam; by 1974 he was chief engineer, and a director of Lotus Cars the following year. He's right at the top now, but that doesn't mean he wants to see Lotus grow too much. Lotus, he says, must stay 'lean and mean'.

He explains the Lotus approach, pointing out that because Lotus is small, it can react quickly. If Lotus Engineering takes on a project for a large, outside manufacturer, he says, it can complete that project in 60 per cent of the time that the manufacturer would need to do the same task itself, and at half the cost. 'We identify the key objectives, and boil them down to first principles. We then start from scratch, with no preconceptions. If the chosen solution is innovative, that's good. We innovate to achieve practical objectives; this is Lotus.' It could almost be Colin Chapman speaking.

'In 1986 we were able, after years of frustrated ambition, to plan long-term for the first time. The results of this are now showing. We were down to 365 people in 1982, but now Group Lotus is 1500 strong. We made around 1100 cars in 1987, and with M100 we'll be up to 3-4000 units a year which is back to late-1960s levels.'

M100 is the final version of X100, which grew out of M90. This car, the new Elan scheduled for launch sometime in 1989, will not after all use a Toyota engine; instead, it will use a 16-valve unit from GM affiliate Isuzu. What's more, it will be Lotus's first front-wheel-drive car. M300, an ultra-high-technology supercar to beat the world, boasting active suspension and possibly a V12 engine, will follow a couple of years later. A Lotus-developed four-cam, 48-valve V12 already exists; it was seen at the 1989 Detroit show in the Cadillac Solitaire concept car.

Lotus profits are now healthy, with Lotus Engineering's consultancy work proving particularly lucrative and the US market growing fast. But the company will not expand: 'We must keep small,' says Kimberley. 'The car company must never go over 5000 units a year.

'It's been a tough road, but a good one; it's tempered the people here. All the engineers we had in 1982 are still with us, though there's been an influx of new blood. We've got solid underpinnings now, and the stability we need for the future.'

Below: 1 1987 Formula 1 Lotus – Type 99. 2 1989 Esprit Turbo. 3 1989 Excel SE. 4 1960 The original Lotus Elite. 5 1966 Lotus Elan. 6 1974 Lotus Europa JPS. 7 1974 Elan Plus 2S/5. 8 1963 Lotus 25. 9 1955 Lotus Eleven. 10 1962 Lotus Seven. 11 1963 Lotus 23. 12 1986 Lotus Esprit Turbo – Limited Edition. 13 1963 Lotus Cortina. 14 1978 *Lotus Elite. 15 1970 Gold Leaf Formula 1 – Type 79. 16 1975 JPS Formula 1 – Type 72. 17 1978 JPS Formula 1 – Type 79. Brought together in 1988, between them these cars represent most of the highlights of Lotus's first four decades. The only notable absentees among the road cars are the Eclat and the Talbot Sunbeam Lotus.*

BUILDING
THE ESPRIT

**From rolls of glassfibre
to 152mph supercar – all
on the same site**

IT'S AN UNLIKELY PLACE for a car factory. Hethel, a short distance south and slightly west of Norwich, is so small it doesn't even appear on some road atlases. Yet, whether by fate or by accident, two of the key players in Lotus's current fortunes bear the names of nearby villages, Kimberley and Spooner Row. The Norwich area is hardly steeped in the car-making tradition, but the local workforce has adapted very well.

Lotus is one of the biggest employers in the area, and prides itself on the flexibility, and quality-consciousness, of its workers. Most people can do most jobs within their section, or can move between sections, and hanging banners throughout the factory remind them that 'Lotus Quality is Everyone's Business'; 'Lotus Quality is Your Job'; 'Lotus Quality is Your Best Salesman'. The message is clear.

Hethel, occupied by Lotus since 1966, used to be an airfield with a few hangar buildings dating back to World War Two. Those buildings, now re-clad and refurbished, are still used today, with more under construction to accommodate the forthcoming M100, or Elan, sports car. Around 80 per cent of the components that go to make up an Esprit are made on site; Lotus might be small, but it's more self-sufficient than many a major manufacturer.

Building an Esprit, or indeed any Lotus, takes around three months' real time and 500 man-hours from roll of raw glassfibre to shining pride and joy. Factory output is currently seven cars a day, with the Esprit Turbo accounting for most of production at the time of writing.

MOULDING THE BODY
Scissors and Stanley knife meet high tech
Glassfibre might be the predominant structural material, but the old-fashioned idea of layers laboriously laid up by hand in a mould, with sticky resin everywhere, is alien to the Esprit's hi-tech image. Instead the Esprit's bodyshell is made by Lotus's own, and patented, VARI (Vacuum Assisted Resin Injection) process. Not only does this produce bodies of much more consistent quality and weight, but it's also much quicker – each mould can produce up to six bodies a day.

For a low-volume, high-quality producer like Lotus, VARI is the perfect way to produce strong bodies with a quality as good as, if not better than, a metal equivalent. Cost is one good reason why: VARI tooling costs tens of thousands of pounds, but tooling for steel bodies costs millions. So how does it work?

The 'outside', or female, mould forms the shape of the body in the usual way, but there's also an 'inside', or male, mould. When the moulds are fitted together, the gap between them corresponds to the thickness of the body, a gap filled with glassfibre and other structural materials, plus the resin which is injected once the moulds are mated. To term the resulting structure, with Kevlar reinforcement of vital areas and foam-filled sill sections, a glassfibre body would be to sell it short: Lotus prefers to call it composite technology.

In fact two pairs of moulds are needed to create a complete Esprit body, because it is made in separate top and bottom halves. The ridge along the car's flanks is more than just a styling feature: it's where the two halves are joined. The previous Esprit model had a similar ridge, even though its body was hand laid. The reason? It, too, was designed for VARI production. However, unlike the Elite, Eclat and Excel, it was never made in that way – which meant that its body thickness could never be as consistent.

Below: The ridge around the Esprit's midriff is more than just a styling feature: it's where the top and bottom halves of the body moulding are glued together, with epoxy resin, in an overlapping join. The joint is then filled and smoothed, with the bonding continuing around the edges of the wheel arches to give great strength. The result is a remarkably sturdy end-product.

*Above: Some of the basic processes of Esprit body manufacture. Making a Lotus starts with cutting pieces of glassfibre and Kevlar, **top left**, using templates to gain the correct shape. These are laid in the female mould, which has been pre-sprayed with a waxy release agent and a gel coat, the male mould is clamped on top, and polyester resin is injected, **top right**, into the space between under vacuum. Once the resin has cured, the raw body shell* *halves are withdrawn from the mould. Later, the top and bottom body halves are glued together, with epoxy resin, **bottom left**, using a bag and nozzle like a giant cake icing applicator. Smaller mouldings are made by traditional hand laying, **bottom right**, because consistency of thickness is less important and small components do not warrant the heavy investment in VARI plant. The extractor vent removes pungent resin fumes.*

CUTTING OUT THE PIECES
Like a dressmaker's pattern

As soon as you enter the body-building shop, you're hit by the smell of resin. But before the resin can play its part in the production process, the many sections of glassfibre mat which are to be laid in the mould need to be cut out using templates, and ensuring the material's 'grain' is the right direction for maximum strength in the finished structure.

Most sections are in simple continuous filament mat, in two or maybe three layers, though woven mat is used for areas where high strength is required, such as in the wheel wells. Even greater strength, where needed, is gained with a combined woven/chopped strand mat. Strongest of all, though, is Kevlar woven aramid fibre, coloured yellow for easy identification, which is used in the roof pillars and around the sunroof aperture. It's so strong that the Esprit can pass all roof-crush and roll-over tests without the need for any steel reinforcement.

Meanwhile, the moulds – each pair is dupli-cated, so two top body halves and two bottom halves can be made simultaneously – are being polished with a release agent, so the resin won't

Top left: Rolls of glassfibre mat, continuous filament or chopped strand, plus yellow Kevlar for highly-stressed areas, is where it all begins. The mat is cut into shapes along its grain, using templates, and stored ready for use. Each shelf is clearly marked to indicate the part of the car for which each piece is intended.

Top right: Here, the female mould for an Esprit shell's top half is being polished with a release agent, so that the gel coat will not stick when it is time to remove the shell from the mould. After this, the next step will be to spray the polyester resin gel coat, which is what gives the body its smooth, shiny, hard outside surface.

Centre left: Next, the pre-cut glassfibre and Kevlar pieces are laid into the mould. Glassfibre rope, or roving, is used to tie together sections which meet at awkward angles. This is the mould for the bottom half; glass-fibre encased polyurethane foam sill members, and the threaded chassis mounting bobbins, go in now.

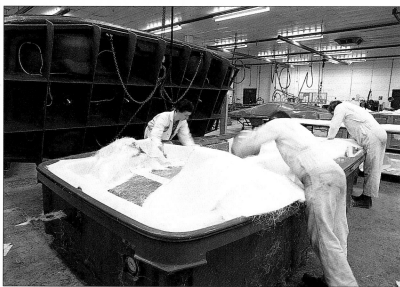

Centre right: Here, the female half of the top mould has been laid up with its glassfibre, and the male half, also polished with release agent, is about to be inverted and clamped in position on top of the female. Resin injection is the next stage; the rubber seal, visible round the mould's edge, helps maintain the vacuum.

Bottom left: An hour after it was injected, the resin has cured and the mould is 'popped' with compressed air to release it from the newly formed body. Then off comes the mould's male half, to reveal a brand new top body section inside. It is still warm from the exothermic resin curing process, but ready to come out.

Bottom right: And out it comes, still floppy at this stage so several men are needed. The new body half is shiny on the outside, but its glassfibre texture shows inside. Its resin thickness is closely controlled throughout, thanks to the precision of the VARI process. Window and door openings will be cut out later.

stick to the mould. Incidentally, the moulds themselves are made using exactly the same composite technology as the bodies they will produce.

INTO THE MOULD
Nature abhors a vacuum

First, a resin and hardener mix is sprayed into the female mould. This will form the smooth, shiny outer surface of the completed body. Then, as this hardens, a team lays the pre-cut pieces of mat into position including the mat-encased foam sill members. Roving, effectively a thin glassfibre rope, is used to tie together angled joins, such as those around the engine and chassis humps, and gives added reinforcement to these potentially weak areas.

The female mould is lowered on to the male mould, and a rubber seal ensures an airtight join between them. Then, through a hole in the male mould in a position where it won't show on the finished body, a powerful vacuum is applied. This is then reduced to an operating level which doesn't distort the moulds, while an extremely sticky machine injects a resin mix from a drum into several different orifices in turn. The vacuum ensures the resin is drawn into every corner and crevice. For the area around the engine bay, a special fireproof resin is used which blends imperceptibly into the normal resin from the next injection point.

About an hour later, the resin has set and the body half is ready to come out of the mould. In a reversal of the earlier process, an air line pressurises the mould and 'pops' it. With the top half pulled off, the air pressure continues; giant air bubbles appear under the translucent moulding, as though under ill-fitting cling film, the shell seems to inflate . . . and out it comes, lifted by a team of maybe eight men. It's still warm; resin cures by an exothermic reaction.

There are, of course, no holes yet: even the window, bonnet and boot apertures are filled in

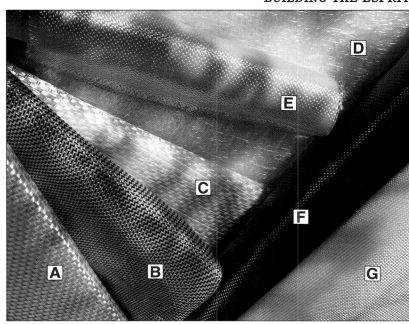

Right: Typical materials used in composite construction. **A** *woven glass (coarse weave);* **B** *carbon fibre/Kevlar aramid fibre hybrid (woven);* **C** *unidirectional glass;* **D** *continuous filament glass (CFM or continuous filament mat);* **E** *woven Kevlar;* **F** *woven carbon;* **G** *woven glass (coarse weave). No carbon fibre is actually used in the Lotus Esprit's body shell, but chopped strand glass mat – not shown here – is employed in certain parts of the structure. Once embedded in polyester resin and thus 'frozen' into position, these materials can form a structure of great strength. Resin-bonded Kevlar and carbon fibre mouldings are especially strong, as well as being incredibly light in relation to their strength.*

by a single layer of mat, and it's here that the round injection aperture marks, like those on the inside surface of a plastic construction kit, can be seen. On the inside surfaces the finish, while smooth and consistent, shows the texture of the glassfibre owing to the lack of a pre-sprayed resin gel coat. Outside, the surface is glossy with just a hint of 'orange peel'; this will disappear as the body is rubbed down between successive coats of paint.

Already the body halves have been given the same identification number, a number which will eventually form the last few digits of the car's ultimate VIN (Vehicle Identification Number, the one that appears in the registration document). As other parts of the car are made, they too will bear that number so that the right assemblies end up in the right Esprit. The progress of each major part of the car, and each team leader's quality checks, will be recorded on Quality Build Sheets

which are brought together as the car takes shape. This way, any problems can be traced right back to source.

VARI is also used for other major mouldings, such as the doors, bonnet and boot lid. However, for smaller mouldings it's more economical, given the tooling costs, to produce them by the traditional hand-laying method. It's a very sticky process, with binnacles, fascia panels, finishers and fuel flaps all produced by a team of men wearing gloves and gel-encrusted aprons. It's rather like an art class. Extractor pipes remove most of the heady resin vapour, and Lotus reports no health (or addiction) problems.

Below: With the top and bottom body halves glued and clamped together, the excess epoxy resin, squeezed out by the clamping pressure, drips out like stalactites. Once the glue has set, the wheel arches will be cut out. Later, with the body moved on to the main fettling shop, the joint flange will be trimmed, filled and smoothed.

THE BONDING SHOP
Two halves make a whole

Here, the translucent top and grey bottom halves of the body are made into one rigid shell. That the two halves have these different colours of gel coat is more a matter of tradition than anything else. If there is a reason, it is that the translucent gel coat makes it easier to see the glass mat patterns when the top half is turned the right way up, while the rough side of the bottom half is facing upwards anyway so the patterns are quite clearly visible.

Strong epoxy adhesive is squeezed, from what looks like a giant cake icing applicator, along the flange around the periphery of the bottom shell moulding. The edges of what will become the wheel arch openings get a further dose. The top half is then lowered on to the bottom half, and a series of clamps squeezes the two halves together amid much dripping of excess epoxy. Then, while the adhesive is hardening, rough access holes are cut in the window and door apertures. This allows a man inside who will bond in the three pieces of seven-ply marine plywood that make up the bulkhead between passenger and engine compartments. Plywood is chosen as a good sound absorber and an effective baffle board for the stereo speakers.

Here, too, the various strengthening webs, dictated by US crash regulations, are bonded into the front boot space of American-market cars. At this point, should a structural fault show up, like a bad crack in the gel coat or worse, the body is rejected and will be cut up so that its good parts can become crash repair sections.

With the epoxy hardened, it is off with the clamps and, with the help of a grinder, off with the joint flange around the midriff of the now one-piece shell. All that's left is the ridge, with any imperfections on its shape to be made good later. The next task is to cut out the wheel arches around a template, which means cutting through the horizontal joint at this point. The outer and inner skins – the inner skin being an upward projection of the bottom shell moulding – are, however, securely bonded together around the wheel arch openings, thanks to that extra dose of epoxy applied just before the clamping stage.

IN FINER FETTLE
The main fettling shop

There's lots of dust (removed by extractors) and lots of activity here. Window, door, bonnet and engine lid apertures are neatly cut; other jigs or templates show precisely the positions of holes for wiring, pipework, ducting and anything else required. Cars for different markets, of course, need different sets of holes, and each set has its own template. For example, a car might have right- or left-hand-drive; it might have marker lights on the sides; it might have air conditioning.

Next, the body, which is starting to look like a proper Esprit instead of an Esprit-shaped blob, is put in an oven to dry out the last of the solvents and to settle its dimensions. Once cool again, the joint seam is filled smooth along with any parts that need to be filled, and once rubbed down it is checked again for inconsistencies.

There's a final filling and flatting session (using Isopon P38, the do-it-yourself body repairer's staple diet), and movable panels – doors, bonnet, engine lid – are selected and honed for a perfect fit. These panels, now matched to the car, stay with the main shell and bear its identification number. The shell is weighed, as a quality and consistency check, after which the two cross-

Above: The translucent body shell looks much less like an amorphous blob once the holes and apertures are cut out. Among the first to be opened up are the wheel arches; the incision is made with a tiny air-powered cutter. Accuracy now saves remedial work later.

Below: In between each of the many coats of paint, be they primer, colour or lacquer, the body is rubbed down and washed to ensure the smoothest finish possible. Surface defects are rectified at once. The final lacquer coat is highly polished, with no 'orange peel'.

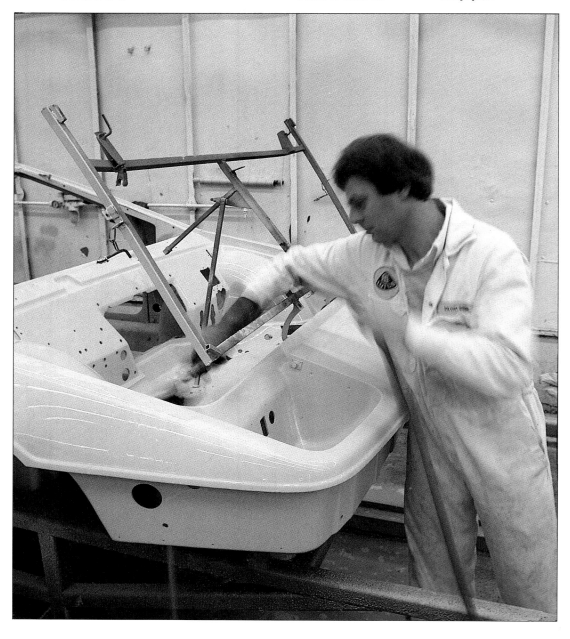

beams are bolted into position.

Apart from the fourteen threaded bobbins incorporated into the body at the moulding stage, to which the chassis will later be bolted, these steel beams are the only metal structural parts in the bodyshell. One fits behind the seats, between two of the pieces of plywood bulkhead, and provides mountings for the door closing plates. The other fits under the scuttle and runs down in front of the doors; it's a mounting for the door hinges, and provides an electrical earth return path for the instruments and switches.

Many of the smaller mouldings are fettled here, too, and fitted to the body. Some are bonded, like the cant rail finishers between the tops of the doors and the edges of the roof, and some are riveted, like the shaped sill covers with their cooling ducts. Finally, a layer of aluminium foil is stuck on the cabin side of the rear bulkhead, as a shield against radio interference.

AND SO TO PAINT
Up to ten coats

There's still some dust in the body's crevices, so it is thoroughly vacuum-cleaned and washed. Once dry, a once-over with a Takrag (literally, a tacky rag) removes any remaining dust, and the first coat of polyurethane sealer can be applied

Once baked in the low-temperature paint oven the body, now all one colour and looking much like pressed-steel with all its holes and fixing points, can be inspected yet again for surface imperfections as it is rubbed down. Three more primer coats follow, each one baked and then rubbed down for a flawless finish, and then it's time for the colour coats.

If the car is to have a metallic or pearlescent finish, there will be two colour coats followed by two dry, dusty coats to make the metallic particles stand out. Two clear lacquer coats then give the glassy, glossy final finish. If it's to be a solid colour, there will be three colour coats followed by the two of clear lacquer. Each is baked and rubbed down, and the last one is then buffed to a high, hard gloss devoid of 'orange peel'.

Lotus uses ICI Autocolor 2K paint, polyurethane-based with an isocyanate hardener to make the paint harden by chemical reaction, rather like an epoxy resin. These two-pack paints release cyanide vapours, which can paralyse a paint sprayer's respiratory system. So the sprayers wear breathing apparatus, and the dangerous vapours are drawn out by extractors in the spray booths.

All the components – doors, for example – that are to be finished in body colour are sprayed at the same time as the main shell, to ensure a perfect colour match.

BUILDING THE CHASSIS
The parts you don't see

While the body is on its seven-week journey from roll of glassfibre to finished, painted and polished shell, other parts of the factory are busy with chassis and engine.

That familiar Lotus backbone chassis starts life as simple sheet and tubular steel, cut and shaped with the aid of a CNC punch/nibbler. There are three main sections, each of which is fabricated separately. Two computer-controlled Trunpf presses, made in Stuttgart, stamp out the smaller sheet steel components.

The front suspension carrier, a simple transverse box section with damper turrets, is one of the main sections; the tubular steel engine cradle

Above: The main shell and its attendant panels, such as doors, bonnet, bootlid or tailgate, are sprayed as one to ensure that all end up exactly the same colour, then they are baked. Then the process is repeated, several times. The shell shown here is actually that of an Excel.

Below: The chassis, fabricated in sheet steel with a tubular engine cradle, is welded together on a jig to ensure accuracy. Once complete, it is sent away to be galvanised. That wide tubular engine cradle was originally intended for Lotus's stillborn 4-litre V8.

is another, with the spine that gives the chassis design its name making up the third. Between the engine cradle and the spine are a wide, angled filler plate and a fillet to fair this into the spine itself.

Each of the three main sections, once fabricated, is placed on a master jig. Minor adjustments, to ensure a perfect fit, are made with the high technology tool known as a hammer. The panel beater's maxim applies here: 10 per cent of wages for hitting it, 90 per cent for knowing where, and how hard, to hit it. With a perfect fit ensured, the chassis sections can be welded together, with seam welding where appropriate, and incorporating the filler plate and spine fillet.

Once completed, the chassis is sent to an

outside firm for galvanising, a process which enables Lotus to offer an eight-year warranty against corrosion. They come back with the characteristically shimmery, shiny finish of a zinc coating, but the heat involved in the process can occasionally lead to distortion. This is checked on a jig, and if the chassis is twisted it is thrown away. It can't be straightened, for to do so would build in stresses. This is one of the reasons why severe accident damage will usually call for a new chassis.

To the bare chassis frame will shortly be added suspension and steering components, all either of cast alloy or cadmium-plated steel, plus the brakes, wheels and – of course – the engine and transmission unit.

THE POWER HOUSE
How the engine is made

The major castings of the all-aluminium engine are cast by outside companies, such as Aeroplane and Motor, but all machining is carried out in-house by Japanese computer-controlled robots – more correctly called a multi-pallet CNC horizontal machining centre. Thereafter each engine is, naturally, hand built but several different technicians will have had a hand in it by the time it breathes its first gulp of air in the test booth. Eight engines a day find their way into production cars; those required for service or parts are made in overtime.

Careful matching of components is vital. The crankshaft, clutch and flywheel are balanced as a unit, and no more than three grams of weight variation is permitted between the heaviest piston and the lightest of the four. Each piston, made by Mahle, comes matched to its alloy cylinder liner, which slides into the cylinder block and is easily removed should replacement eventually become necessary. The inside surface of the liner is coated with Nikasil, a nickel/silicon compound very good at resisting wear.

With all its intricately ribbed aluminium castings, this is a fine looking engine. Even the sump is of cast aluminium, while the exhaust manifold's voluptuous curves terminating at the turbocharger, and the purposeful looking stubby inlet tracts from each carburettor venturi, almost flaunt the engine's potency.

Once built, the engine is wheeled into a test cell. There, it is run for an hour to loosen it up, so a technician can set the carburation and ignition. To begin with, the engine is run at 1000rpm for 10 minutes, then at 2000rpm for the same time, and finally at 3000rpm, by which time it's running freely enough for the subsequent adjustments to be valid. It won't happen to normal production engines, but development engines on the test bench under load can produce so much heat that the exhaust manifold and turbocharger glow red.

Frank Harris, Lotus's long-serving engine test

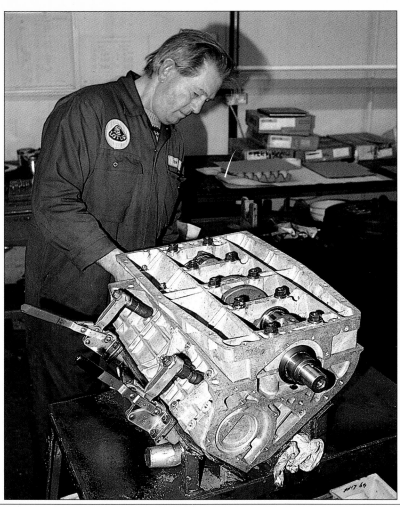

Above left: An Esprit Turbo engine nears completion, with just the camshafts, cam covers and carburettors to go. *Above right:* The Mahle pistons are supplied complete with their removable, Nikasil-coated aluminium, wet cylinder liners; here, the fitter is working on the oil pump. *Below left:* Assembling the engine block; main bearing plate is visible. *Below right:* Finally, the finished engine is mounted in the chassis.

Left: Newly built engines are run in the test cell for an hour, building up the speed in gentle stages. Then, with the engine's initial stiffness easing off, the carburettor and ignition settings are carefully checked and adjusted, and any faults which have shown up can be put right.

expert, points out that it's far better for any engine faults to show up under bench testing than in the car, because it takes sixteen hours to take an Esprit Turbo's engine out of the car and put another one back in!

Once set up, the engine is mated to its Renault UN1-16 transaxle, and the engine/transmission unit is then ready to slot into the chassis.

FINAL ASSEMBLY
On down the line

The assembly line, which accommodates Esprits and Excels alike, begins at the point where chassis meets body. Now complete with engine, the fully-built rolling chassis is pushed to the start of the line, picked up by an overhead winch and lowered on to a four-poster hydraulic lift, which is itself in its lowest position. The body, already fitted with water radiator, oil cooler, air-conditioning condenser, fans, wiring, wiper spindles, vertical rear window and some sound deadening, is then hoisted by a second winch into position above the chassis. It is lifted by its wheel arches, specially moulded load spreaders/lifting eyes hooking exactly into position around them without damaging the paintwork. Many other specially moulded protection panels will be used further down the line.

Next, the body is lowered, nose down, on to the chassis, and stout mounting bolts are screwed

Below: The final result, Lotus's turbocharged powerhouse sits snugly in this red Esprit's engine bay. Regular service items are fairly accessible, apart from the distributor which is buried under the carburettors, but it takes sixteen hours to remove and replace the engine.

Left: The most dramatic moment of all is when the body meets the chassis; the Esprit becomes an entity at last. The cables of the *overhead winch are hooked into moulded protection plates to prevent body damage. The new assembly line is seen in the distance.* *Above: An Esprit's leather trim starts off as coloured cowhide from Connolly Bros. Scandinavian cows are best; they are less prone to skin* *tears and parasite damage. Different parts of the hide are used for different parts of the trim, according to the degree of stretch required.*

through holes in the chassis into some of the body's mounting bobbins. This is the point at which the collection of components truly becomes a Lotus Esprit Turbo, when body and chassis become one.

There are more mounting bolts to fit from underneath, so the ramp is raised to the level of an elevated section of assembly line. There's more underside work to do now, as the car is slowly pushed to the end of the elevated section, then another ramp brings it down to ground level again for the rest of the components to take their place in the new car.

SUB-ASSEMBLIES
The efficient way

More and more use is being made of sub-assemblies, themselves put together at stations alongside the appropriate part of the assembly line and built in to the car complete. Thus the deformable bumpers, foam-filled for the US, have their lights pre-mounted, the instrument binnacle contains all its VDO instruments fully tested, and the doors are fully assembled with an extruded aluminium side impact beam, the winding window and the electrically heat-bonded quarter-light glass. Current is applied to a thin wire running through the rubber/mastic sealing strip, and the heat cures the rubber.

The biggest sub-assembly station is the trim shop, where the Esprit's interior is expertly fashioned from soft leather and luxurious cloth. A hive of industry with a heady smell, a mixture of leather and glue, it's the only section of the manufacturing area that is partly a ladies' domain.

It is here that the glassfibre fascia and instrument binnacle, or some of the many small ABS plastic components made in Lotus' own vacuum-forming plant, are covered in leather or cloth as required. And it's here that foam rubber, in a variety of densities depending on where it is to be used, meets steel frame and cowhide to make up the seats. Six or seven Scandinavian cows will have given up their skins for an Esprit with full leather trim, skins which will take on one – or two, depending on the model variant – of a dozen standard colours, or any other colour to order. You want a lime green leather interior? No problem: it can be done.

The leather comes from famous English curriers Connolly Brothers, who favour Scandinavian cows for their reduced tendency to suffer tears and parasite damage. Which part of the hide is used for which part of the interior is critical; the skin along the animal's spine stretches in two direction, so it's no good for seats as they would quickly become baggy looking.

Above: Once cut to shape, the pieces of leather, or cloth if applicable, are sewn together as required. Then they are ready for covering the foam-filled seats and other interior panels elsewhere in the trim shop. A heady smell, a mix of leather and glue, pervades the atmosphere.

Below: The end of the line draws near. Here, the windscreen is about to be fitted; with this done, these Esprits will be very close to completion. A few final checks remain, plus a shakedown run on the test track, and the new Lotuses are ready for their owners.

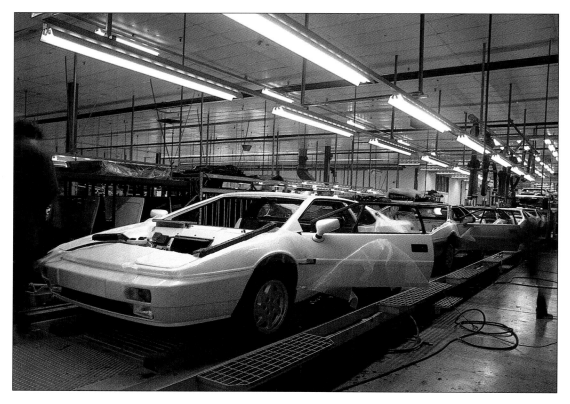

THE END OF THE LINE
Ready for delivery

By the time the new Esprit has reached the wall separating the factory floor from the engineering research offices, it's complete and ready to be moved over to the final inspection bay. Here, the end product of those 500 man-hours will be surrounded by Lotuses bound for all over the world, all showing subtle differences to suit them to their eventual destination. Although the Lotus range nominally consists of four basic cars – Turbo Esprit, normally aspirated Esprit, Excel and Excel SA with automatic transmission – there are nine distinct body specifications and seven different engines.

After a thorough check by white-coated inspectors, it will move under its own power for the first time as it sets off for road test on the factory's 2.4 mile test track just across the road from the main buildings. Then, with any necessary adjustments completed and the Quality Build Book signed for the last time, the Esprit is ready for its eager new owner. Those three months of waiting are over at last.

LOTUS ENGINEERING
Expertise with confidentiality

Building supercars is far from being the only thing that happens at Hethel. It's also the home of Lotus Engineering, a separate company within Group Lotus headed by Tony Rudd, which was set up in 1980. Its turnover has increased fivefold between 1982 and 1987.

Lotus Engineering, as well as being Lotus Cars' research and development department, is a highly respected, brilliantly innovative engineering consultancy whose services are sought after by clients throughout the motor industry and beyond it. Currently, 105 projects are under way for sixty-four clients whose identity is guaranteed to remain anonymous if the client so wishes.

Mike Kimberley sees Lotus cars as a good advertisement for Lotus's engineering consultancy – and the research generated by clients' projects rubs off on future Lotus cars, which in turn make ever better advertisements. It's the perfect support for the Lotus image of high technology, and it means that Lotus engineers can develop far more expertise than they would ever be able to do were Lotus a car manufacturer alone.

And there are more engineers, too. In 1977, when consultancy work began as a separate entity, there were forty-three engineers. Now there are 860, more than in some large car companies.

PROJECTS: CLIENTS AND LOTUS
In the forefront of technology

Some of Lotus Engineering's past projects are well known. They include turbocharging the MG Metro, developing the suspension of the Volvo 480 and improving the handling of the Isuzu Piazza Turbo (which wears *Handling by Lotus* badges). But, as well as projects for specific clients, Lotus Engineering is highly committed to its own research.

The best-known fruit of this is Active Suspension, first looked at, and then dropped, by Team Lotus in 1982 and then adopted by Lotus Engineering. Much was written in the mid-1980s about the black Esprit Turbo Active Suspension development car; research, carried out in conjunction with several other manufacturers, continues and the system could well see production in Lotus's top-range M300 model, slated for launch in a couple of years' time. Put simply, Active Suspension dispenses with springs and, instead, actively moves the wheel up or down according to the forces acting on it and the programming of the control computer.

Another intriguing area is Anti-Noise – the technology of exactly matching a sound with the same sound transmitted out of phase, thus cancelling the original sound out. Connect one of the speakers of your stereo the wrong way round, and you'll find the volume of the bass notes is reduced; this is the principle behind Anti-Noise.

Other research areas include composites technology, in which Lotus's expertise is obvious, styling by Lotus Design (we've seen how both the Esprit and the Excel were styled in-house), electronics – plus, of course, Lotus's famed ability in engine and suspension design. The Lotus emissions

Left: The Millbrook test track, near Ampthill in Bedfordshire, is probably the best vehicle test facility in the UK. The high-speed bowl is clearly visible in this picture, with the acceleration straight to the left and the handling circuits within the bowl, adjacent to the steering pad. In the foreground the hill route can be seen.

laboratory and evaporative emissions test facility is one of three in Britain recognised by the US Environmental Protection Agency and the European and Japanese authorities, there's an advanced NVH (noise, vibration and harshness) laboratory, and the engine test suite contains eight test cells. Lotus Engineering can even, if asked, take on an entire car project from drawing board to production-ready state.

One of Lotus Engineering's most notable successes has been the VARI technology, now licensed to users throughout the world. It's as good an illustration as any of the Lotus tradition of innovation; of defining the objectives, going back to first principles, and innovating to find a practical solution. As Mike Kimberley says, 'This is Lotus'.

THE GENERAL MOTORS CONNECTION
. . . or lack of it

General Motors owns Group Lotus, and has done since January 1986, but apart from wishing to ensure the Group's profitability it takes no part in the running of the constituent companies. Lotus Engineering's guarantee of client confidentiality is cast iron, for the simple reason that if a GM rival found that GM had knowledge of the rival's project with Lotus, that rival would take its business elsewhere – maybe to 'our friends at Weissach', as Mike Kimberley refers to Porsche's research and development centre.

In fact, that Lotus retains its own identity, control structure and client confidentiality is enshrined in an agreement between GM and Group Lotus, and reinforced in a letter from Robert J. Eaton, GM vice-president, to Mike Kimberley. It's the logical approach; one of the main reasons GM wanted to buy Lotus was for the Hethel company's engineering expertise and consultancy business. Now, the idea is to expand this business; with GM's financial muscle, and the chance of recruiting the best people that this allows, the only way is up.

MILLBROOK
Britain's best test track

One of the first signs of this expansion was Lotus's recent purchase of the 700-acre Millbrook Proving Ground near Ampthill, Bedfordshire, from the now defunct Bedford Trucks arm of General Motors. A full research centre in its own right, which continues to carry out contract work for other divisions of GM, the proving ground has a high-speed bowl two miles in circumference, acceleration straights, two handling courses, dirt roads and much more. It's regularly used by other British car manufacturers, as well as by the majority of British motoring magazines, who are sworn to secrecy over what they might see . . .

With Millbrook among its assets, Lotus Engineering is truly on the map. The future is looking good for this jewel of automotive high, and British, technology.

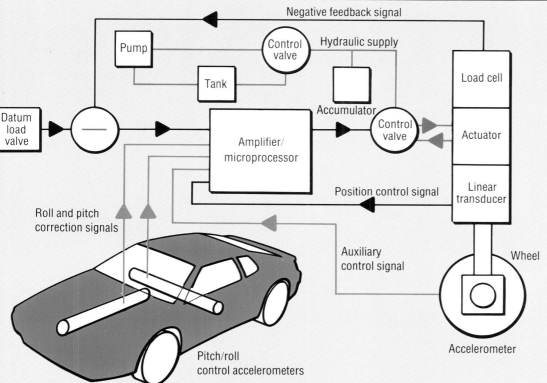

Negative feedback signal · Pump · Control valve · **Hydraulic supply** · Tank · Load cell · Accumulator · **Datum load valve** · Amplifier/ microprocessor · Control valve · Actuator · **Roll and pitch correction signals** · **Position control signal** · Linear transducer · **Auxiliary control signal** · Wheel · **Pitch/roll control accelerometers** · Accelerometer

LOTUS ACTIVE SUSPENSION SYSTEM

Above: Lotus's Active Suspension system replaces conventional springs with hydraulic actuators. When the load cell at the top of the actuator senses a greater than normal load, such as would happen when the wheel hits a bump, it sends a signal to the central computer which then commands the actuator to shorten itself. This is achieved via the actuator's control valve, which signals the hydraulic pump to suck fluid out of the actuator. This makes the piston – and hence the wheel – move up to accommodate the bump.

This effect, or the reverse if the wheel encounters a dip, happens within milliseconds. A transducer, attached to the actuator piston, measures the speed and distance of movement, and through a feedback system it ensures that the wheel movement is correctly damped. Should the load persist for more than, say, 30 seconds, the system treats it as the new norm – a built-in self-levelling device to compensate for extra weight.

There are two further accelerometers, one to measure the forces of braking and acceleration, the other to measure cornering forces, which also feed their signals into the computer. Using this information, the computer can be programmed to adjust the actuators to compensate for squat under acceleration, dive under braking and body roll when cornering. The need for firm suspension, usually required for the best roadholding so that the suspension geometry remains correct, is thus banished at a stroke; the suspension can be as soft as you like. With Active Suspension, you can have your cake and eat it.

DRIVING THE ESPRIT TURBO

Turn the key and the Lotus comes alive, with telepathic handling, awesome performance and inimitable style

IMAGINE YOU'RE MEETING a brand new Lotus Esprit Turbo for the first time. Your mind might experience floods of conflicting emotions: pride that the Lotus is British, prejudice that this sleek, exotic-looking supercar doesn't have an Italian pedigree. Excitement and wonder at the performance promised from its 2.2-litre (133cu.in.), turbocharged four-cylinder engine; disappointment that there aren't six, or eight, or even twelve cylinders with the glorious howl of a potent, naturally aspirated power unit.

Is it better than a Ferrari or Porsche? Or worse? Or just different? Examine it closely, then drive it, and you'll see that such judgements are irrelevant: the Lotus Esprit Turbo is a unique, an exhilarating and quite wonderful companion. Lotus's maxim is Handling, Performance & Style. The Esprit Turbo is living proof.

THE FIRST LOOK
Excitement unbounded, trepidation unfounded
To one unfamiliar with it, the Lotus Esprit looks to be a daunting machine to drive. It's wide, low, squat and broad-shouldered. How do you get into it without contorting muscles you never knew you had? And, once in, how do you see out of it? Rest assured. It may be a supercar, but it's a benign one.

First, a closer look outside. Those lines, as curvaceous as the previous model Esprit's were angular, give the Lotus a purposeful unity of form that hints at power but doesn't shout it. You know that this is, first and foremost, a driving machine, but creature comforts, and as much practicality as a mid-engined two-seater will allow, have not been overlooked.

As for quality of construction, the Esprit is wanting for little. The paint is flawless, the attention to interior detail buries once and for all the stigma of Lotus's 'kit car' heritage. This is a Lotus in maturity, a top-flight sports car to compete on level terms with the best.

Yet there are niggles. The gaps between the plastic body panels, though consistent, are wide; and they look the wider because the body moulding process leaves some panels with overly rounded off edges. It's the only external clue to the way the body is made. Strange, too, are the blank triangular sections immediately ahead of the front quarterlights, which look as though they should house the door mirrors. That, originally, was the intention, but European mirror legislation meant that a mirror so mounted would need to stick out unacceptably far if it was to give a sufficiently wide field of view. So why not paint the triangle black?

On the nose is the latest design of Lotus badge, a reversion to the original style of Colin Chapman's era except that the letters are now serifed. Move round to the flanks, and you'll see a Lotus Design badge just behind the front wheel arch where Giugiaro's signature used to be on the old car – and why shouldn't Hethel's design studio be proud of its work? Further towards the back, behind the door, is the subtlest of Esprit Turbo lettering, directly above a formidable air scoop in the sill.

Open the door, and slip inside. You'll need to thread your legs round the handbrake as you step over the wide sill, for it sticks out of the inside part of the sill just ahead of the front of the driver's seat. When not being pulled, the handle lies flat whether the handbrake is on or off, just as in a Ferrari or a Jaguar XJ-S, but you're still liable to trip over it.

Before you shut the door behind you, take a look at the door hinge. It's a huge, solid-looking galvanised affair with an earthing strap for the door's electric mirror and central locking, spelling out sturdiness and security. Then, with door pulled shut (and try to forget that the interior door handles are vintage British Leyland, still used because they do the job well) and you can relax in your cockpit, almost as though in a motoring cocoon.

Snug, yes; claustrophobic, no. Claustrophobia went out with the old-shape Esprit Turbo, a car with a high scuttle, an eye-level steering wheel and minimal rearward vision through its layers of rear cooling slats. It's different now. You still sit low and laid-back, in a seat whose backrest angle is now, at last, adjustable, and the body sides still edge up to shoulder height or beyond, but no longer do the steering wheel and the boomerang instrument binnacle thwart the view forwards for those not endowed with long backbones.

Look into the rear view mirror, and there's a better view than you might expect through the tunnel atop the engine. That sloping tailgate

Below: The view as you open the door. The leather-covered, thick-rimmed, three-spoke steering wheel is good to hold, with the ends of the upper spokes turned down for a comfortable quarter-to-three grip. Behind it lies a comprehensive array of white-on-black instruments.

glass, though, unique to the Turbo Esprit and covering only the top two-thirds of the distance from roof to rear spoiler, acts like a mirror itself. If your Esprit is a red one, the glass positively glows as it reflects the red paint of the bodywork beneath it, causing a red cast in the top half of the interior mirror's field of view. But most of the time it's not a problem, and there are always the large door mirrors, electrically heated and adjustable with Citroën-sourced switches, to fall back on.

Rear three-quarter vision, the sort you need when looking over your shoulder to exit from an acutely angled junction, is better than you would expect through the rear quarter windows. So often this is a problem in mid-engined sports cars, but less so in the light and airy Lotus.

READY FOR ACTION . . .
. . . in a well-planned driving environment
It's a good driving position, just right for fast, confident progress. The seat, with its prominent side bolstering, lacks support under the thighs for the taller driver, which is strange given Mike Kimberley's lofty build. But it promises to clamp its occupant firmly during spirited cornering, and on the whole it does; even if it didn't, you couldn't slide far to your left because there's a high, wide barricade to stop you. Within it, beneath soft leather-covered padding and a layer of glassfibre, lies the chassis backbone, so high that its top forms a convenient elbow rest. The gear lever, with its Renault knob, protrudes barely 5in. (127mm) above it.

Your feet operate pedals which are offset to the left, a result of the front wheel arch's intrusion

into the cockpit. Otherwise they are positioned well, with the accelerator close enough to the brake to allow the side of the shoe to blip the throttle for a smooth, synchronised-speed downchange while the ball of the foot is pushing the brake pedal. You don't notice the offset after a while; there's also a rest for the left foot.

Look forward, and you see nothing of the Esprit's nose, so steeply does it slope. You'll soon discover, though, that this is not the slightest impediment to driving, to placing the car through gaps. Only when parking in a tight space will you have to indulge in a bit of inspired guesswork.

DOWN TO THE DETAILS
A closer inspection
Lower your gaze slightly, and take in the contents of that bold, boomerang-shaped binnacle. The instruments are German-made VDO ones now, but they are small and their individual glass lenses, though given non-reflective surfaces, catch the light badly from certain angles. It's a shame that the two dominant dials, the speedometer and tachometer, weren't made bigger and easier to read, as befits such a fast car, while the interior was being redesigned. It's a pity, too, that the whole instrument panel wasn't covered by a single, horizontally-concave, non-reflecting glass in the modern idiom.

Between the two major dials, and sharing their

Above: A Clarion stereo nestles above the heating controls, whose panel is shared by lettering which reads, in a throwback to the previous model, Turbo Esprit instead of Esprit Turbo. A Renault gear knob, comfortable to grip, betrays the transmission's origins.

Below: At rest in the flat lands of its native Norfolk, sun low in the sky, the Esprit Turbo seems impatient to be on the move again, to get on with the serious business of fast driving on challenging roads. The 1987 re-design has given the Esprit a much brawnier, more muscular feel.

white-on-black calibrations and black bezels, lies a turbocharger boost gauge directly ahead of the driver's nose with a digital clock beneath. To the tachometer's left, and slightly below, is an oil pressure gauge with a voltmeter further to the left again. To the speedometer's right you'll find the water temperature gauge with the fuel gauge beyond; your view of both the fuel gauge and the voltmeter is obscured by the steering wheel rim. There's no doubt that the traditional looking dials are a part of the Esprit's sporting Britishness, notwithstanding their German manufacture, but ergonomically they are not the best.

No such criticism applies to the chunky, leather-covered steering wheel with its thick rim and three stubby spokes. The upper pair curve down for a perfect fit around the thumbs, with a palm sized bulge in the rim just above for those who favour a ten-to-two grip instead of a quarter-to-three. Just 14in. (355mm) in diameter, it's good to look at, equally good to hold and bears a proud Lotus emblem in its padded centre.

But it bears no horn push; this is to be found on the end of the left-hand steering column stalk, a stalk which also dips and flashes the retractable headlamps, and actuates the indicators. Its counterpart on the right controls the single pantograph windscreen wiper, designed to sweep right up to the right-hand pillar, and the windscreen washer. You'll find Fiat stalks in a Ferrari, so Lucas items lifted from a British Leyland (or Rover Group) application are understandable in the Lotus.

Britain's biggest motor manufacturer also provided the source for the rest of the fascia switchgear – three push/push buttons on the left of the boomerang to operate sidelights, headlights and heated rear window, another three on the right for hazard flashers and fog lamps for front and rear. Move your left hand down to the centre console, and you'll find rotary controls for the heating system, and the air conditioning if fitted. Above it sits the stereo radio/cassette player, a fine Clarion system with four speakers – two on the rear bulkhead behind the seats, and one at each end of the fascia.

Next to the right-hand edge of the seat, recessed into the sill, your right hand will find a pair of levers for the electrically actuated fuel filler flaps, one on each side of the car. They each belong to their own, separate tank, but the tanks are connected by a balance pipe – as I discovered the first time I filled an Esprit to the brim with fuel. The Lotus was parked on a sloping forecourt so that one filler was lower than the other. Both fillers were open, and I was pumping petrol through the higher one first, intending to continue with the other once the first was full, as you would with, for example, an old-shape Jaguar XJ6. The inevitable happened. As quickly as fuel went into the upper filler, it poured out of the lower one. An expensive mistake on my part; I should only have had one filler open at a time. Next time I'll read the handbook . . .

Another lever, near your right shoulder and accessible only when the driver's door is open, releases the twin catches of the rear tailgate. Once open, this reveals a boot plenty big enough for a well-dressed couple's weekend luggage, and a fibreglass cover in front of it; lift this off to find the engine beneath. If you see an Esprit with

scrapes at the top of the tailgate, it's because its owner forgot to close the sunroof before gaining access to the boot or the engine. This, too, is spelt out in the handbook.

You pull a rather crude wire loop under the fascia to open the front bonnet, but there's not much baggage space beneath; for the brake servo, spare wheel, radiator and fuse boxes have staked a prior territorial claim.

IRON FIST IN A VELVET GLOVE
The Esprit Turbo comes alive
There's a choke knob below and to the right of the steering column, but you don't need to use it unless the weather is very cold. A couple of dabs on the accelerator, in the time-honoured fashion of twin-choke sidedraught Dellorto and Weber carburettors, suffices to give the engine the rich mixture it needs to start from cold. What you *don't* do is pump the pedal before a hot start, for

that will almost certainly flood the engine.

Cranked over a few compression strokes by the powerful pre-engaged starter, the engine bursts into life with an eager buzz and ticks over evenly, untemperamentally. There's the distant whine of the camshaft drive belt, the rustling of sixteen cold tappets, the deep but slightly flat hum of the exhaust. Blip the throttle and there's a muted version of the hard, hammery, hollow induction snort so characteristic of a full-house Ford Escort rally car, the induction snort only an engine with one carburettor venturi and a short induction tract per cylinder can utter. Why muted? Because there's a sound-absorbing turbocharger between the source of the snort and your ears.

Right: Apart from the colour, the 40th anniversary Esprit's most obvious visual change is the rear wing above the tail spoiler. The first 88 new-shape Esprits sold in the US were also white, and bore this same wing design.

Right: This is Mike Kimberley's personal Esprit Turbo, one of a batch of forty special edition cars produced to celebrate Lotus's 40th anniversary. The bodywork is finished in pearlescent white, with wheels painted to match the body instead of their usual silver finish.

That blip on the throttle has an instantaneous, almost electric response, better than that of any fuel injection system because those fat Dellortos force a healthy squirt of neat fuel down those stubby induction tracts each time the throttle is pressed. Will it be as eager when we're on the move, when the engine has the load of the car to drive and perhaps some turbocharger lag to overcome?

Let's find out. Clutch down, and into first gear. Considering the power it has to transmit, it's a light clutch; letting it up, it proves itself to have a smooth, well-cushioned but positive bite. With the engine warmed through, we can give it its head; accelerator foot down, a gentle surge almost instantly becomes the clamp of a giant hand pinning you to the seat, 7000rpm on the tachometer and time for second gear.

The lever slots into second, clutch up and full throttle again. There's a perceptible delay, then a distant whistle builds up as quickly as the boost gauge needle shoots up its scale. The whistle is quickly followed by a loud sucking sound, the sound of air being sucked through the air intake at the back of the quarter window a couple of feet behind your right ear, before being compressed by the ever faster spinning Garrett T3 and forced through those four fat carburettor venturis. Such sounds, magnified tenfold with the side window open, are denied to drivers of left-hand-drive Esprit Turbos. They're sitting in front of the wrong air intake.

In a trice the 7000rpm rev limit, guarded by a cut-out to prevent engine damage, is upon us again. Lift off the throttle pedal, ready for the upchange, and as with the previous upshift your right ear is assailed by a whistly rat-tat-tat, a sound like that of a hissing rattlesnake. This is the wastegate fluttering, bouncing, as it dumps the excess of compressed air that has nowhere to go while the four throttles are closed. On up through the gears, now; 7000rpm in second gear corresponds to 67mph (107kph), just 3mph short of a UK blanket speed limit that seems so

Above: Compared with the old Esprit's, the new car's interior is much more integrated looking. The 'boomerang' binnacle is solidly mounted, and contains neat push/push switchgear. Stereo speakers sit at the base of the windscreen.

pointless, so irrelevant when there exist cars of the Esprit's towering ability, and there are still three more gears to go. Using all 7000 available rpm, third gear will take you to 99mph (159kph), fourth to 131mph (210kph), fifth, giving 23.7mph (38kph) per 1000rpm of engine speed, will not allow the engine past about 6500rpm . . . which corresponds to 153.5mph (247kph).

That is the speed achieved by the test staff of the highly regarded *Motor* magazine in their road test car. It was a speed, moreover, achieved not in a straight line but around Lotus's own Millbrook high speed bowl with the consequent loss of a few mph in tyre scrub – yet it was still 2mph faster than the factory claims for UK-specification cars. It was complemented by acceleration times that were similarly claim-beating.

AWESOME ACCELERATION
Five seconds to 60mph

That was the startling figure recorded by *Motor*'s car, 0.3sec better than Lotus expected. To beat that you'd need to be driving a Lamborghini Countach, or something impossibly exotic like a Ferrari F40 or a Porsche 959. There can surely be no faster accelerating four-cylinder production car (except the brand-new Esprit Turbo SE, for which Lotus provisionally claims a completely startling 4.5sec to 60mph (96kph), 11.2sec to 100 (161kph), and a top speed of 170mph (273kph).

Achieving this degree of acceleration calls for the best possible getaway. You hold the engine at approximately 4500rpm, let the clutch in smartly and feed in exactly the right amount of throttle. The rear wheels spin, smoke pouring from the sticky Goodyear tyres as the car hurtles forward, and road speed finally catches up with the engine whose speed has never dropped below the

Above right: The Lotus Esprit Turbo in its element, on a twisting, challenging secondary road. With its tremendous roadholding, surprisingly forgiving handling and the ability to catapult out of corners and on to the next straight, the Esprit Turbo is a formidable ally.

4250rpm maximum torque point. Then it's into second, then third, then fourth . . .

You'll never need to be this brutal on the road, but carried out at the test track this routine sees 30mph (48kph) in an astonishing 2.0sec, the quarter-mile marker in 13.7sec having already reached 100mph (161kph) in 12.6sec (Lotus claims 14.7), and the kilometre in a stupendous 24.9sec.

Powerful adjectives, yes. But the Lotus deserves them, for there is precious little that can stay with it in performance terms. Was *Motor*'s car tweaked? Certainly it proved the quickest of the road test cars, but those of other magazines have all emulated it in making the manufacturers's performance claims look conservative. I drove *Motor*'s car, E324 TAH for number-plate watchers, and I'd say it was representative enough.

Something which intrigued the testers at the time was this: the new Esprit Turbo, despite having the same 215bhp engine as its immediate predecessor and weighing 88lb (40kg) more, was 10mph faster flat out and 0.4sec quicker to 60mph. The only differences were gearing – apart from the identical first gear ratio, the new car is slightly longer-geared – and the new car's apparently superior aerodynamics, though Lotus was claiming a drag coefficient as low as 0.33 for the final old-shape Esprit Turbo. As we have seen, though, Peter Stevens has revealed that the old car's true drag coefficient was actually over 0.40. Puzzle solved.

Right: Pausing for a moment at Lotus's Hethel test track, the Esprit bathes in the evening sun before certain rain. On wet roads, the Lotus becomes notably less forgiving of error in its handling, with its tail apt to slide on a wet bend should you snap the throttle shut or accelerate too hard. Quick reactions and the concentration accorded any supercar are needed to catch it.

POWER WITH FLEXIBILITY
A stunning mid-range, too

The Lotus 910 turbocharged engine positively rockets to its rev limit, with an almost uncanny smoothness as it does so, but that is not to suggest it is lacking in urge at lower speeds. True, its maximum torque of 229lb ft isn't liberated until a relatively high 4250rpm, but the torque curve is quite a flat one and there's 180lb ft on tap as low as 2000rpm.

Provided, that is, that the turbocharger is already spinning quickly and boost is building up. In practice, normal driving doesn't see the turbocharger blowing hard until around 2500rpm, though the build-up of boosted power is delightfully progressive. Mind you, it's not so progressive that you would ever forget that this is a turbocharged engine, for you are always aware of a slightly soft throttle response under load, a little lag before things really start to happen; but the fact that the Lotus is turbocharged is hardly ever a handicap. The sabre-sharp throttle response of a Porsche 911 or a Ferrari 328, the crisp, immediate reaction to the slightest change in throttle pedal position, is missing except when idly blipping the throttle at tickover – but does it matter?

When the Esprit can post 20mph incremental acceleration times in fourth gear, from 40 to 60mph (64–97kph) through to 80–100mph (129–161kph), of between 4.2 and 4.6sec, arguably it does not. A similar argument goes for fifth gear: from the 50–70mph (80–113kph) increment through to the 80–100mph (129–161kph) one, none takes over six seconds and the last mentioned needs just 5.8. So a little lethargy

before the boost comes on stream (20–40mph (32–64kph) in fourth gear takes 8.1sec, in fifth 11.2sec) can be forgiven. If you want more go, you change down; it is no hardship, for the gearchange, while a touch rubbery, is fast, short in its throws, quite precise and meaty enough to complement the Lotus's feeling of potency.

Yet some would say, when the sensations of a supercar are under scrutiny, that the way of doing something is more important than what is done. And here, the Lotus could lose friends. That softish throttle response is one reason. The noise, notwithstanding the excited whooshes from the turbocharger, is another; the eager exhaust rasp, characteristic of a 16-valve four-cylinder engine, is ever-present but it's a rather flat, shallow sound compared with the excited scream of a flat-six Porsche in full cry, or the exultant blare of a Ferrari V8. But never mind. The Esprit Turbo will out-accelerate both – and it's hard to imagine what other production car could even get close to the Lotus Esprit Turbo SE. Remember, too, that it's all from just 2.2 litres . . .

HANDLING: AS GOOD AS THE BEST
Fine-honing means driver delight

Few cars can scuttle round corners as quickly as a Lotus Esprit Turbo. The sheer cornering forces it can generate are phenomenal, yet they are easy for the driver to exploit. Such is the essence of a Lotus. This is where the company has always excelled.

The car's rearward weight bias, inherent in its mid-engined design, is balanced by the larger footprint of the rear tyres, and by front suspension geometry designed to encourage the front wheels to run wide, or understeer, at high cornering speeds which would otherwise see the heavier rear end stepping out of line first. The result? A near-neutral cornering stance; the car corners with the precision and directional control of a slot racer right up to near-impossible speeds.

Below: On the left are power and torque curves for the UK-specification Esprit Turbo with Dellorto 45M DHLA carburettors. On the right are those for the normally aspirated Esprit, which *shows a 'peakier' power curve; it rises at an increasing rate and then drops off abruptly. In the Turbo the fall-off is more gradual, the torque is concentrated further down the engine speed range.*

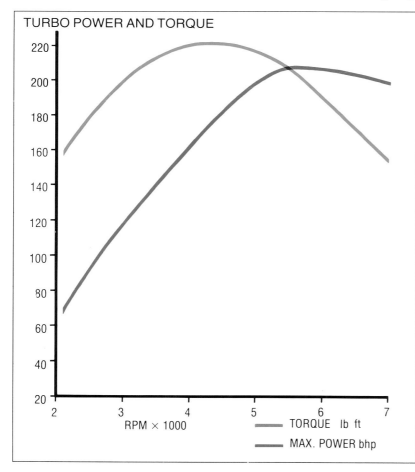

TURBO POWER AND TORQUE

RPM × 1000

TORQUE lb ft
MAX. POWER bhp

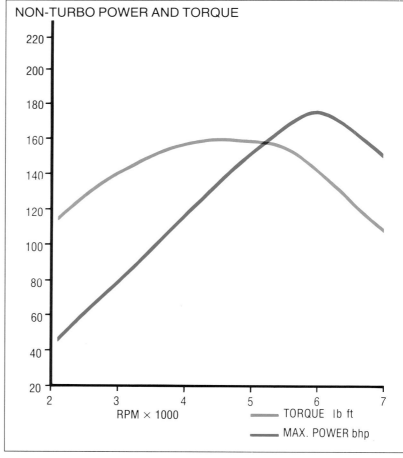

NON-TURBO POWER AND TORQUE

RPM × 1000

TORQUE lb ft
MAX. POWER bhp

Above: The polarised light of early evening highlights the Esprit's curves to perfection, and shows just what Colin Spooner means by 'surface orientation'. Less flatteringly, it also highlights the rounded-off edges of the body panels. The author spent a thrill-packed week with this car, F235 XNG, during research for this book.

Below: In a high-speed action photograph like this, in which the detail becomes blurred, the thrusting form of the wedge shape becomes even more apparent. Peter Stevens deliberately made his Esprit more masculine than Giugiaro's car; the maestro approves of Stevens' remodelling, but considers it too close to the original.

Above: The chargecooled, 264bhp, 163mph Turbo SE runs on wider, lower-profile tyres, revised front suspension geometry, stiffer front springs and gas-filled dampers. Handling and grip are even better than before.

Below: Within the confines of the Hethel test track, the Esprit Turbo can be given its head. A startlingly rapid car it may be, but it is also docile in temperament, easy to drive and not in the slightest bit intimidating.

Right: Induction and cooling air is sucked into these purposeful looking scoops, and intriguing sounds emerge from the upper one. When the throttles are snapped closed, there is a whoosh and a rattle like a rattlesnake hissing.

Roger Becker, general manager and chief engineer of vehicle development, says the Esprit is not a car for fools. It is designed to feel as though an extension of the driver; it is a car developed by keen drivers for keen drivers to appreciate. With its mid-mounted engine, the weight is concentrated in the middle which gives it a low polar moment of inertia. Put more simply, this means that not much effort is needed to make the car change its direction, even though the total weight of the car is quite high.

You could liken it to a fighter aircraft, designed deliberately to be unstable so that it can change direction instantly. That said, for a car to be driven safely as well as quickly by people of common enthusiasm but widely differing levels of skill, it is necessary to build in some degree of failsafe stability. That's why the understeer is there; the Esprit, Becker suggests, might give a warning snap if provoked too far, but it won't actually bite you.

The other, and purer, way of ensuring the car stays safe is to give it even more grip. This is the approach used in the Turbo SE, which runs on wider, lower-profile, 50 per cent aspect ratio tyres and is designed to understeer less. It also has lighter steering, a more progressive transition into its eventual tail-out attitude, and its cornering stance is more sensitive to the amount of power being fed to the back wheels. In other words, it will prove to be an even more rewarding car for the very skilled, though the unwary might initially find it less reassuring.

But back to the regular Turbo, a car with a chassis so capable you wonder how it *can* be bettered. Its stability is tremendous, achieved in

part by giving the steering a relatively large castor angle and, consequently, making it quite heavy. The chargecooled car has less castor; in the standard car, you curse it at low speeds or when parking because it makes the steering a true biceps-builder. As the speed goes up, though, the steering needs much less effort, and the merest twist of the wrist is enough to flick that invisible nose on to a different course.

The speed of the steering's response (quicker than the 3.0 turns lock-to-lock would suggest), and the precision and determination with which the nose bites into the bends, are among the Lotus's greatest assets – though that castor means the more subtle messages from the road surface are not transmitted to the steering wheel's rim as faithfully as in some supercar rivals. This responsiveness, plus superb damping of body movement, makes the Esprit the greatest of companions along a challenging, twisting, sinuously snaking secondary road; it feels, as its designers intended, an extension of your senses. It simply goes round corners, and very quickly, the body staying almost flat as those fat tyres bite into the road. You seem to have to do no more than *think* it round a bend, as you squeeze on just the right amount of power for a slingshot exit on to the next straight.

If you power too fast into a bend, the lightly laden nose is pushed wide by the thrust from the rear and the steering, which normally gets heavier as the cornering load increases, will go light. You simply slow down, and the nose comes back into line. If you're more adventurous, though, you can accelerate instead; the tail will edge out and the car will fly through the bend in a pulse-racing drift, perfectly balanced or, if you're feeling extrovert, with a final tail flick and a

Left: At over six feet wide, 73.2in. (1860mm) to be precise, the Lotus can be a tight fit in a country lane; it is bigger than it looks. Tinted glass, instead of body-colour glassfibre, is optional for the removable, tilting sunroof.

Above: *Night puts paid to the sleek contours of the Esprit's nose, for it is then that the headlamp pods have to be raised. The outer lights are for dipped beam, with the inner pair joining in for main, or high, beam.*

touch of corrective opposite lock from the driver.

But beware. On tighter corners or on wet roads, where the understeer can build up more quickly given the chance, the transition from understeer to oversteer can be an abrupt, sudden one and you need to be quick with the steering to catch the tail, even if you've done nothing more than lift off the throttle as you turn in. The Lotus will react quickly, with none of the swinging-on-a-pendulum sensation of the tail-heavy, tail-happy Porsche 911, but you must react quickly too.

CIVILISED EXCITEMENT
A remarkable ride

Once you know the Esprit, it's a forgiving enough car which allows you to explore its limits in a way you might not dare in a 911 or a Ferrari 328, despite their lighter, more communicative steering less blunted by castor. It's a car which will let you relax if you are not in the mood for on-the-limit heroics, for you know it's not going to catch you out without warning you first.

In a gusty crosswind, the sort that has a 911 trying to switch motorway lanes as if it had a

Left: *Esprit of the water waves, beachcombing on the Norfolk coast. Colin Chapman used to own the Moonraker yacht company whose boat hulls were made, like the Esprit's body shell, by Lotus's VARI process.*

mind of its own, the Esprit tracks straight and true. On a bumpy road, the suspension soaks up bumps and undulations almost as a luxury car would, supple springing combining with tight damping to banish all unwanted body movement. At low speeds, you can certainly feel the small bumps of a pock-marked road, but only enough to remind you that you are in a taut, sporting car. Harsh the Lotus never is; the great rigidity of the new body, on the same chassis as before, means that the current car can be sprung more softly than its predecessor yet lose nothing in road-holding. Colin Chapman would have approved, for this is precisely what he was always aiming to achieve.

In the way it stops, too, the Esprit inspires confidence. Those big disc brakes haul the Lotus down from very high speeds with no fade and no drama. They feel as though they could stop a train. Make them a little less hyper-sensitive to light pedal pressures, a little less snatchy when stroking the brakes to check the car's progress at lower speeds, and they would be perfect. There is no anti-lock system as yet, but premature locking of the lightly laden front wheels – the bane of many a mid- or rear-engined car in the past – simply doesn't happen.

So, capable of generating raw excitement, or of cossetting its driver after a hard day's brainwork, the Esprit Turbo has matured into a refined and covetable car. It isn't even noisy any more. Wind roar used to be a problem in the old body shape, and the engine contributed its share of aural input, but nowadays the air slips past with barely a sound and the engine's song has retreated backstage. Much of the time, it's the rumble of tyre treads over coarse road surfaces that dominates, and even that never obtrudes to excess.

A LOTUS FOR THE 1990s
Post-GM maturity encapsulated

The Lotus Esprit Turbo, with its smooth new suit of clothes, its searing performance (with more yet to come), and its coherent blend of superb handling, supple ride and impressive refinement, represents perfectly the new face of Lotus. From pure sports cars long on driver appeal but short on durability, through a push upmarket into GT territory and an image problem, to today's sophisticated drivers' cars and a burgeoning reputation for technological prowess, Lotus has grown up. For the Hethel company, life is truly beginning at forty.

If the Esprit Turbo, now with a decade and a half of development behind it, has become a fully paid-up member of the supercar club, then the chargecooled Turbo SE surely deserves a place on the committee. What's more, the two turbocharged Esprits arguably remain Britain's only affordable supercars, for the Aston Martin Virage is priced at stratospheric heights and we have yet to see how Jaguar will pitch the forthcoming F-Type.

The final question, though, must be: *does* an Esprit Turbo truly present a convincing alternative to the charismatic rivals from Maranello and Stuttgart-Zuffenhausen, the Ferrari 328 and the Porsche 911? A couple of years ago, when the old-shape Esprit was current, I would have said not. Now, the answer is an unequivocal yes. Lotus has got there at last.

LOTUS ESPRIT
Specifications

T=Turbo
US=Federal Turbo
NA=normally aspirated Esprit

Engine	Configuration	In-line four-cylinder, mounted longitudinally behind cockpit and ahead of rear wheels, type 910 (T/US), 912S (NA)
	Construction	All-alloy
	Capacity	2174cc (132.7cu.in.)
	Bore	95.3mm (3.75in.)
	Stroke	76.2mm (3.00in.)
	Compression ratio	8.0:1 (T/US), 10.9:1 (NA)
	Main bearings	Five
	Max. engine speed	7000rpm
	Normal idle speed	950 ± 50rpm
	Maximum power	215bhp (160kW)/6000rpm (T) 228bhp (170kW)/6500rpm (US) 172bhp (127kW)/6500rpm (NA)
	Specific power	99bhp (73kW) per litre (T) 105bhp (77kW) per litre (US) 79bhp (58kW) per litre (NA)
	Power/weight ratio	170bhp/tonne (T) 180bhp/tonne (US) 146bhp/tonne (NA)
	Maximum torque	220lb ft (298Nm)/4250rpm (T) 218lb ft (295Nm)/4000rpm (US) 163lb ft (221Nm)/5000rpm (NA)
	Firing order	1-3-4-2

	Valve gear	Four valves per cylinder, twin overhead camshafts driven by toothed belt, bucket tappets
	Valve clearance, cold inlet:	0.005–0.007in. (0.13–0.18mm)
	Exhaust:	0.010–0.012in. (0.25–0.31mm)
Cooling	Type	Closed circuit, water-cooled. Thermostat opens at 82°C (175°F)
	Radiator	At front, twin electric cooling fans. Separate header and expansion tanks in engine bay
	Capacity	2.6 gallons (12 litres), pressurised at 1.0bar (15psi)
Fuel system	Type	Dual Dellorto 45M DHLA (T) or 45D DHLA (NA) twin-venturi sidedraught carburettors, or GM MPFI multipoint electronic fuel injection with full engine management (US)
	Turbocharger	Garrett AiResearch T3, with water-cooled bearing and integral wastegate (T/US)
	Fuel capacity	Two tanks, 17.3 gallons (78 litres) total (T/US), 14.7 gallons (67 litres) total (NA)
Electrics	Ignition system	Lucas breakerless electronic (T/NA). Fully-mapped within MPFI engine management (US)
	Ignition advance	10° BTDC at idle
	Spark plugs	NGK BPR6EY (T/US) NGK BPR7ES (NA)
	Plug gap	0.9mm (0.035in.)
	Alternator	Valeo 90 amp
	Battery	Tungstone 088, 330 amp cold start
	Fuses	36
Lubrication	Type	Wet sump, pressure pump and oil cooler
	Oil capacity	1.43 gallons (6.5 litres)
	Oil pressure, hot	Not below 0.3 bar (5psi) at idle 2.4 bar (35psi) at 3500rpm 3.1 bar (45psi) at 6500rpm
Transmission	Transaxle	Renault UN1-16 all-synchromesh
	Oil capacity	0.66 gallons (3.0 litres)
	Recommended oil	Mobil SHC 630M
	Internal ratios and mph/1000rpm	1st – 3.36:1/5.8 2nd – 2.05:1/9.5 3rd – 1.38:1/14.1 4th – 1.03:1/18.7 5th – 0.82:1/23.7
	Reverse	3.54:1
	Final drive	3.88:1
	Clutch	Single dry plate 9.25in. (235mm) diameter, diaphragm spring cover assembly, hydraulic operation
Suspension	Front	Independent by upper and lower wishbones, anti-roll bar, co-axial coil springs and telescopic dampers
	Rear	Independent by upper and lower transverse links, semi-trailing radius arms, co-axial coil springs and telescopic dampers

Steering	Type	Rack and pinion, end-mounted track rods
	Ratio	15.4:1
	Turning circle	36ft (11.0m) between kerbs
	Turns lock-to-lock	3.0
Brakes	System	Bendix master cylinder, direct-acting vacuum servo, dual circuit split front/rear
	Front	Toyota ventilated discs, 10.1in. (258mm) diameter. 0.8in. (20mm) thickness
	Rear	Bendix solid discs, 10.8in. (275mm) diameter, 0.5in. (12mm) thickness
	Handbrake	Operates on rear calipers by cables
Wheels/tyres	Front wheels	OZ Italia 7-spoke alloy, 7JK x 15in.
	Front tyres	Goodyear Eagle NCT
	Size	195/60 VR15
	Front pressure	1.5bar (21psi)
	Front camber angle	0° 30′ negative ± 0° 30′
	Front castor angle	min 1° 45′, max 3° (within 0° 30′ side to side)
	Front wheel toe-in	0.06in. (1.6mm) each side +0, −1.0mm)
	Kingpin angle	9° 23′ nominal
	Rear wheels	OZ Italia 7-spoke alloy, 8JK × 15in.
	Rear tyres	Goodyear Eagle NCT
	Size	235/60 VR15
	Rear pressure	1.7bar (25psi)
	Rear camber angle	0° 30′ negative ± 0° 15′
	Rear wheel toe-in	0.06in. (1.5mm) each side ± 0.5mm
	Spare wheel/tyre	Pressed steel rim, 175/70 SR 14 Goodyear Grand Prix S tyre, max. speed 50mph (80kph)
	Spare pressure	2.0bar (30psi)
Structure	Chassis	Galvanised steel backbone, forked ends to accommodate front suspension and tubular engine/ rear suspension carrier
	Body	Composite moulding in bonded upper and lower sections, produced by vacuum-assisted resin injection (VARI)
Dimensions	Length	170.5in. (4330mm)
	Width	73.2in (1860mm)
	Height	45.3in. (1150mm)
	Wheelbase	96.0in. (2438mm)
	Front track	60.0in. (1524mm)
	Rear track	61.2in. (1554mm)
	Ground clearance	5.8in. (146mm), driver only aboard
	Kerb weight	2793lb (1268kg) (T/US) 2593lb (1177kg) (NA)
	Weight distribution	43 per cent front 57 per cent rear
Performance[1]	Maximum speed	152mph (245kph) (T) 155mph (249kph) (US) 138mph (222kph) (NA)
	0–60mph (97kph)	5.3sec (T) 5.2sec (US) 6.5sec (NA)
	0–100mph (161kph)	14.7sec (T) 12.7sec (US) 18.8sec (NA)

Performance[2]	Maximum speed	153.5mph (247kph)
	Maximum in fourth	131mph (210kph)
	in third	99mph (159kph)
	in second	67mph (107kph)
	in first	41mph (65kph)
	Standing starts:	
	0–30mph (48kph)	2.0sec
	0–40mph (64kph)	2.8sec
	0–50mph (80kph)	4.0sec
	0–60mph (97kph)	5.0sec
	0–70mph (113kph)	6.7sec
	0–80mph (129kph)	8.3sec
	0–90mph (145kph)	10.3sec
	0–100 (161kph)	12.6sec
	0–110mph (177kph)	15.5sec
	0–120mph(193kph)	18.8sec
	Standing quarter mile	13.7sec
	In fourth gear:	
	20–40mph (32–64kph)	8.1sec
	30–50mph (48–80kph)	6.0sec
	40–60mph (64–97kph)	4.6sec
	50–70mph (80–113kph)	4.2sec
	60–80mph (97–129kph)	4.2sec
	70–90mph (113–145kph)	4.4sec
	80–100mph (129–161kph)	4.4sec
	90–110mph (145–177kph)	4.4sec
	100–120mph (161–193kph)	6.7sec
	In fifth gear:	
	20–40mph (32–64kph)	11.2sec
	30–50mph (48–80kph)	9.6sec
	40–60mph (64–97kph)	7.3sec
	50–70mph (80–113kph)	6.0sec
	60–80mph (97–129kph)	6.0sec
	70–90mph (113–145kph)	6.0sec
	80–100mph (129–161kph)	5.8sec
	90–110mph (145–177kph)	6.5sec
	100–120mph (161–193kph)	7.3sec
Consumption	Urban cycle	16.5mpg (T) 17.6mpg(NA)
	At 56mph (91kph)	33.9mpg (T) 40.7mpg (NA)
	At 75mph (121kph)	26.6mpg (T) 33.9mpg (NA)
	EPA city driving	17mpg (US)
	EPA highway driving	28mpg (US)

[1] Official Lotus figures.
[2] UK-specification Esprit Turbo figures obtained by *Motor* magazine, week ending 21 May 1988.
All other specifications are as issued by Lotus.

INDEX

PICTURE CREDITS
The publishers wish to thank the following photographers and organisations who have supplied photographs for this book:

**General Motors
Corporation:** 23 (bottom)

Ital Design SpA: 14 (bottom), 15 (top)

Brian Laban: 12

Lotus Cars Ltd: 16 (bottom), 17, 18, 24, (bottom) 27 (top left and right), 62

Lotus Engineering: 20 (top), 25, 26 (cutaway) 27 (bottom), 32 (bottom), 39 (top)

Millbrook Proving Ground Ltd: 47 (top)

**Monitor Press Features
Ltd:** 4 (bottom), 5, 6, 8, 10, 11, 16 (top), 34 (bottom)

Performance Car: 56 (top)

Quadrant/Autocar: 9 (cutaway), 13, 14 (left), 15 (bottom)

Renault UK Ltd: 31 (cutaway)

All other photographs in this book, including endpapers and cover illustrations, were taken by **Jim Forrest.**

The editor is also grateful to the following for their help and kind cooperation:
Michael May, Chris Groom and Alastair McQueen at Lotus; and Bernard Usher at Monitor.